András Kraft

Time in Byzantine Apocalyptica

CHRONOI

Zeit, Zeitempfinden, Zeitordnungen

Time, Time Awareness, Time Management

Edited by
Eva Cancik-Kirschbaum, Christoph Markschies and Hermann Parzinger

on behalf of the Einstein Center Chronoi

Volume 23

András Kraft

Time in Byzantine Apocalyptica

DE GRUYTER

ISSN 2701-1453
ISBN 978-3-11-223010-7
e-ISBN 978-3-11-223011-4 (PDF)
e-ISBN 978-3-11-223012-1 (EPUB)
DOI https://doi.org/10.1515/9783112230114

Library of Congress Control Number: 2026932003

Bibliographic information published by the Deutsche Nationalbibliothek
The Deutsche Nationalbibliothek lists this publication in the Deutsche Nationalbibliografie; detailed bibliographic data are available on the internet at http://dnb.dnb.de.

De Gruyter and Walter de Gruyter GmbH are part of De Gruyter Brill.
www.degruyterbrill.com

Questions about General Product Safety Regulation:
productsafety@degruyterbrill.com

Contents

Acknowledgments

The distinction between time (χρόνος) and timing (καιρός) is fundamental to Greek thought. It draws on the difference between the quantitative aspect of duration and the qualitative notion of a propitious moment. The dichotomy applies well to the present work, which required both sustained institutional support and timely collegial advice to explore the notion of time in Medieval Greek apocalyptic literature. It was written during a year-long fellowship at the *Einstein Center Chronoi* and was completed while in residence at *Dumbarton Oaks*. I am deeply grateful to both institutions for their support. I am especially thankful to the *Einstein Center Chronoi* for facilitating access to Greek manuscripts from the *Ambrosiana Library*. I am equally indebted to Andrei Timotin for his assistance in studying manuscripts housed at the *Romanian Academy Library* and to Father Theologos for providing unfettered access to codices at the *Monastery of Ivērōn* on Mt Athos. I owe a collective debt of gratitude to the many colleagues who supported this work. In particular, I would like to thank Paul Magdalino and Panagiotis Theodoropoulos for their discerning feedback and suggestions. I also wish to express my gratitude to Stefanie Rabe for the encouragement to publish this work in the Chronoi series and to Franziska Küster for her meticulous editorial work. Finally, I must recognize the unflagging patience of my wife Anna, who endured the untold demands of this monograph with Stoic grace.

Dumbarton Oaks, New Year 2026

https://doi.org/10.1515/9783112230114-001

Prolegomena

Nella profezia è implicita sempre una teologia della storia.[1]
Agostino Pertusi

The Eastern Romans cultivated a critical interest in eschatological matters. This was partly due to the fact that the Scriptures and the Church tradition were purposely reticent about the fine points of eschatology. Decisive questions about the timing, order, and process of end-time events were left open by the biblical canon and its authoritative exegetes. To fill this gap, late antique and medieval authors produced a wide range of pseudonymous writings that professed to uncover the providential chronology and geography of the impending end times. Some of those compositions presented forecasts concerning the political fortunes of kings and empires, while others disclosed insights into the fate of the souls of the deceased. The different perspectives resulted in two divergent yet related literary groups: historical apocalypses (also called political prophecies) and moral apocalypses (also labeled otherworldly journeys).[2] The bifurcation of apocalyptic literature corresponds to the inherently binary character of the apocalyptic imagination, which expects the gradual dissolution of the world and envisions the creation of another in its stead.

Historical apocalypses are primarily concerned with time-bound events in this world. They construct histories of the future. Moral apocalypses, in contrast, are preoccupied with the otherworldly experiences of divinely allocated recompense and retribution. They explore the topography of the afterlife and are largely spatial, rather than temporal, in focus. While heavenly journeys provide valuable correlative evidence for how the Eastern Romans conceived of worldly time,[3] political prophecies are more revealing and thus constitute the main focus of the present study.

1 Pertusi 1979, p. 46.

2 This categorization is based on the classical definition of the genre "apocalypse" by Collins 1979, p. 9. For a succinct characterization of the two subgenres, see Collins 1996, who is followed by DiTommaso 2005, pp. 195–196. On Byzantine historical apocalypses, see Alexander 1985, Pertusi 1988, and Guran 2014. On moral apocalypses in Byzantium, see Baun 2000, Baun 2007, pp. 30–33, and Neil 2016.

3 Regarding the perception of time in moral apocalypses, see Röckelein 1998, pp. 150–153 and Baun 2007, pp. 144–147.

https://doi.org/10.1515/9783112230114-002

Studies in Byzantine apocalypticism have enjoyed increasing popularity over the past decades.[4] Medieval Greek prophecies have been scrutinized for new, otherwise unknown historical information, following in the footsteps of the pioneering work of Paul Alexander.[5] Moreover, apocalyptic scenarios have been explored for their influence on historical developments and political decision-making.[6] This fact-oriented, historicist approach is certainly valid, but it does not exhaust the range of possible approaches that lend themselves to Byzantine apocalypticism. Apocalypses can also be studied for their literary, linguistic, cultural, and aesthetic properties. This book investigates them from a literary standpoint, highlighting characteristics that concern the concept of time. Hitherto, only a handful of studies have been dedicated to Byzantine notions of time,[7] and even fewer works have examined how the Eastern Romans portrayed temporal processes and qualities in anticipation of the Last Judgment.[8]

This study reconstructs key aspects of apocalyptic time insofar as they can be ascertained from historical prophecies originating during the Byzantine millennium (c. 500–1500 AD). It comprises a literary analysis in three chapters, which explore the chronology, velocity, and typology of Medieval Greek apocalyptic narratives. The narratological chronology of the end times forms the subject of the first chapter. It is followed by a discussion of specific phenomenological aspects of apocalyptic time. Lastly, the third chapter exposes the towering significance of typological exegesis. The ultimate purpose of this investigation is threefold. First, it aims to advance our understanding of the intricate interplay of Byzantine histo-

4 Modern scholarship on Byzantine apocalyptic literature began in the late nineteenth century, when German (Bousset 1895, Kampers 1896, Sackur 1898) and Russian (Istrin 1897, Vassiliev 1893, Veselovskij 1875) scholars examined Greek, Latin, and Slavonic versions of Byzantine apocalypses. Arguably, the interest of those scholars reflected the political atmosphere on the eve of the First World War. In the aftermath of the defeat of the German and Russian empires, scholarly interest in apocalypticism abated. It was revived in the second half of the twentieth century by Podskalsky 1972, Alexander 1985, and Pertusi 1988, whose works remain foundational. It is noteworthy that scholars who wrote as recently as 20 years ago felt the need to include an apologetic note, justifying the study of Byzantine apocalyptic literature (e.g., Brandes 2003, p. 70, Treadgold 2004, p. 237, Magdalino 2005, p. 41, Brandes 2007, p. 259). Today, such vindication is no longer needed.

5 Alexander 1968. For two exemplary case studies, see Alexander 1973 and Kaegi 2000.

6 For pertinent case studies, see Treadgold 2004, Magdalino 2007a, and Kraft 2021a.

7 See the collection of papers in Leroux 1984, pp. 419–488 and Saradē, Dellaporta, and Kollyropoulou 2018 as well as the studies by Podskalsky 1990, Ciolfi 2018, Koder 2019, Boudreau 2023, and Çelik 2023. Recently, scholars in related fields (e.g., Geppert and Kössler 2015 and Rothauge 2017) have called for a "temporal turn" in historical research. This book takes up the call, albeit in a preliminary fashion.

8 See Rydén 2000 and Betancourt 2016. The present work revises and resumes material from four earlier studies of mine: Kraft 2017, Kraft 2018b, Kraft 2018c, and Kraft 2018d, pp. 78–123.

riography and apocalypticism. I hope that the reconstruction of the literary substructure of Medieval Greek apocalypses further strengthens the historicist approach in properly decoding instances when historical references lie embedded in apocalyptic literature. Second, the study seeks to shed new light on the Byzantine theology of time, which encompasses a range of cultural and intellectual components, not the least of which is the apocalyptic tradition with its portentous horizon of expectations.[9] Third, the book emphasizes the literary value of apocalyptic narratives and promotes their standing as literature.

Historical apocalypses can be considered a kind of historiography.[10] They construct histories of the future that typically consist of two sections: a historical review with numerous *vaticinia ex eventu* (retrospections presented as prophecies) and a predictive forecast with genuine prognostications. Both sections draw on a preexisting set of motifs, text-blocks,[11] and typological patterns. The dividing line between historiography and actual prophecy is not always easy to discern, which makes dating apocalyptic texts a difficult task.[12] This is equally true of moral apocalypses, which present timeless truths that are particularly hard to date by internal evidence alone. External evidence, such as manuscript transmission, is often of limited help, given the fact that most manuscripts containing Medieval Greek apocalypses were produced in the post-Byzantine period.[13] Fortunately, the precise dating of each apocalypse is of little relevance to the present study, which reads the source material holistically and from a trans-epochal perspective. The exact dating of individual texts does not affect the overall argument of this study.

More severe challenges to the literary analysis presented herein are posed by the fragmentary evidence, the predominantly late text tradition, and the general reluctance among the Eastern Romans to theorize about apocalyptic time. It is thus necessary to excavate the often tacit presumptions from the sources and to rely on secondary evidence. Alexander Kazhdan and Giles Constable have laid out the need to adduce indirect evidence in order to overcome the scarcity and

---

9 For discussions of the theology of time in the medieval West, see Le Goff 1960, Keller 1996, pp. 84–139, and Schmidt-Biggemann 2004, pp. 327–441.

10 Al-Azmeh 2004, p. 200 astutely suggests that apocalypses advance ideal-type notions of history.

11 On the notion of text-blocks, which are larger, coherent units of literary motifs, see Pogossian and La Porta 2017, p. 825. Text-blocks function as compositional elements that can be reshuffled and modified. Like scriptural pericopes, they communicate a coherent idea with multiple propositions and semantic layers.

12 Guiding principles for dating historical apocalypses are presented in Kraft 2012, pp. 215–216.

13 See Brandes 2005, p. 462 and Kraft 2018a, pp. 141–143.

the restrains of the extant sources.[14] With this in mind, the Medieval Greek apocalypses examined here are supplemented with testimonies in related genres, including historiographical, hagiographical, and patriographical accounts.

Certain aspects will not be discussed in this study. Non-revelatory prognostic texts, such as astrological or oneirocritic treatises, are not considered here, as they belong to different literary genres and rely on an epistemological authority distinct from that of revealed prophecies. Furthermore, the technical aspects of time reckoning (horology) in Byzantium will not be addressed.[15] This is not to deny the importance of practical matters, but those aspects do not fall within the domain of apocalyptic discourse. Another important aspect that will not be discussed for the same reason is the liturgy. It is no exaggeration to say that the liturgical experience influenced virtually every aspect of Byzantine life, including the perception of time.[16] Through habituation and practice, the liturgy taught that quotidian time belongs to the worldly existence of transient change and continuous becoming.[17] At the same time, it imitated and rehearsed the divine suspension of temporal divisions by making Christ present in the Eucharist and by typologically re-enacting biblical events.[18] The towering significance of liturgical orthopraxy is acknowledged but will not be explored in this study.

A few remarks on terminology are in order. I use the terms 'eschatological' and 'apocalyptic' largely synonymously. Technically speaking, 'apocalypticism' forms a subgroup within the larger field of 'eschatology'. 'Apocalypses' can be defined as literary compositions that appeal to a revelatory authority and relate to either this-worldly or otherworldly events (following Collins' classical definition) in such a way that they impart an eschatological trajectory and, concurrently, possess the chronotopic characteristic of suspending spatiotemporal boundaries and emulate prototypical texts, such as the canonical *Book of Daniel*, or *Revelation*, or the apocryphal *Apocalypse of Ps-Methodios*.[19] In contrast to the circumscribed do-

14 Kazhdan and Constable 1982, pp. 162–178, 202–204.

15 For the classical heritage and Byzantine use of public clocks, see Landels 1979, Schreiner 1989, pp. 500–505, and Anderson 2014. On timekeeping and time division in Byzantine society, see Grumel 1958, pp. 161–180, Rautman 2006, pp. 3–8, Demandt 2015, pp. 331–334, and Koder 2016, pp. 49–51.

16 For an overview of the development of the Byzantine Rite, see Taft 1992.

17 On liturgical time, see Angenendt 1998, Louth 2009, Louth 2013, Gador-Whyte 2017, pp. 147–154, and Boudreau 2023, pp. 118–214.

18 See Ozoline 1990, pp. 139–140 and Krueger 2014, pp. 75–105.

19 The aspect of chronotopicity will be discussed below in chapter 3. On the importance of prototypical texts, see Newsom 2005. Both canonical and paracanonical texts could serve as prototypes to Byzantine apocalypses. This inclusive approach entails that apocalypses as a literary

main of 'apocalypticism', 'eschatology' is an umbrella term that covers anything that relates to the end of times. That said, the two terms are used interchangeably hereafter, given that any study on apocalyptic literature is inherently also a study on eschatology. I also use the terms *eschaton* ("last", "final") and *synteleia* ("consummation") often synonymously, although a distinction can certainly be drawn. Under *synteleia* I understand the threshold that delimits this world from the afterlife, while *eschaton* signifies the end times broadly understood, including the post-apocalyptic realm. This subtle difference in meaning does not influence the analysis that follows and will thus not be maintained consistently. Furthermore, I adopt the label "apocalyptica" from Lorenzo DiTommaso, who introduced it in order to designate apocalyptic texts collectively, without recourse to any specific text tradition, language, or genre.[20] Accordingly, I use the label "apocalyptica" to refer to the plethora of apocalyptic sources as a group.

Byzantine apocalyptica were potentially accessible to all strata of society and thus counted among the most inclusive kinds of literature in Byzantium. Apocalypses were of universal interest, as they commented on the exigent socio-political issues of their intended audiences. The comments were placed into a biblical exegetical framework that was designed to temper anxieties and foster visions of hope. The language register of those prophecies is, for the most part, a low variety of written Medieval Greek, which emulates the Koinē of the Septuagint and the New Testament.[21] At times, it even approximates the vernacular of the spoken language. The low language register enabled any Greek speaker to understand the wording—if not the meaning—of a given prophecy. In addition, the rhythmic and melodic prose, the visual allusions, and the familiar biblical frame of reference were widely popular. The comprehensibility and aesthetic appeal made Medieval Greek apocalypses a popular and pervasive literary genre.[22] Accessibility to apocalyptic literature was curbed, however, by imperial censorship. The claim to have access to the ultimate truth about the last days made apocalyptic prophecies a potent means for promoting or inhibiting political change. Hence, apocalypses could be either submissive to or seditious against the *status quo*. While pro-imperial eschatology approved of the current establishment, anti-imperial eschatology

---

genre have indistinct or fuzzy margins. See Kraft 2020, pp. 174–178. On a different note, I do not consider urgency (or immediacy) an indispensable feature of apocalyptic literature.

20 DiTommaso 2005, pp. 94–95.

21 Notable exceptions are the *Prediction of Ps-Brysōn* and *Oracles of Leo the Wise*, which are written in classicizing verse.

22 Baun 2007, pp. 102, 264, 369 and Hatzopoulos 2011, pp. 112–114.

sought to subvert and overthrow it.[23] State authorities promoted the former and harshly penalized the latter.[24] Consequently, apocalyptic literature was an inherently ambivalent genre in Byzantium.

Ambivalence is a recurring theme that runs through all three chapters of this study. Ambivalences are found in the chronology, velocity, and typology of apocalyptic prophecies. While the contents and significance of key eschatological events were generally agreed upon, the sequence and timing of those events were a matter of constant uncertainty. Likewise, the commonly held belief that time would speed up towards the *eschaton* was tempered by literary techniques that suspend uncontrollable acceleration through temporal irregularities and the deferral of the end. Moreover, typological patterns, which form the backbone of Byzantine apocalyptica, are marked by deliberate axiological ambivalence. Types that appear identical in content and form are all too often revealed to hold contradictory values and meaning. As will become apparent, ambivalence is a core feature of Byzantine apocalypses.

The present study itself maintains an ambivalent position, which I shall clarify at the outset. In the following, I remain uncommitted regarding the veracity of the apocalyptic narratives under scrutiny. It does not matter for the present analysis whether the apocalypses were the products of genuine revelation or mere wishful thinking. Either view is a possibility, and this work takes no position on the matter. The fact that much of Byzantine apocalyptic literature has been falsified by the course of history does not invalidate its claim to divine revelation. Indeed, apocalyptic visions retain their revelatory authority even when unrealized if their purpose is to provoke a historical shift through repentance (cf. Jer 18:7–8). Conversely, the mere claim to revelatory authority does not exempt those texts from the suspicion of being driven by mundane interests only. Neither of these views is endorsed or rejected. The intentionally agnostic and ambivalent stance regarding prophetic authenticity and veracity adopted in this study is intended to prioritize the literary analysis of the textual corpus.

---

23 For the use of pro-imperial eschatology in Late Antiquity, see Shoemaker 2018. On anti-imperial eschatology in Hellenistic Judaism, see Portier-Young 2011.
24 See Brandes 2008.

1 Chronology

In a word, Byzantium never really got over the fact
that the world did not end with the Arab conquests.[25]
Paul Magdalino

The consummation of the world was assumed to correlate with the end of time. This assumption was rooted in ancient philosophy, which understood time to be ontologically dependent on the divine paradigm of eternity, on the one hand, and to be a function of worldly motion and change, on the other.[26] Accordingly, once change ceases to occur in the post-apocalyptic age, time effectively ceases to exist. Thus, it is hardly surprising that apocalyptic literature, when exploring time-related aspects, focused almost entirely on the events that precede the consummation. This meant that any description of apocalyptic events was temporally confined by the consummation (or *synteleia*), naturally prompting the Eastern Romans to inquire *when exactly* it would occur. Attempts to establish its timing either proposed a precise date or identified specific events and their sequence, which needed to unfold beforehand.[27] The duality of date-based and event-based apocalyptic predictions persisted throughout the Byzantine millennium. The Eastern Romans made ample use of both approaches but generally fa-

---

25 Magdalino 1993, p. 31.

26 The *locus classicus* is Plato's *Timaeus* (37c–38c), where time is defined as "an eternal image that moves according to number" (κατ' ἀριθμὸν ἰοῦσαν αἰώνιον εἰκόνα, 37d6–7), whereby the number (day, month, year) is established by the motion of the celestial bodies. Plato presented time as a deficiency inherent in the physical world, as it is unable to accommodate the atemporal eternity of the intelligible forms. The dichotomy between cosmic time and divine eternity became a philosophical principle, reiterated throughout the centuries by figures like the fourth-century scholar-bishop Eusebius, *De laud. Const.* VI.3–4 (pp. 206–207) and the thirteenth-century erudite monk Nicephorus Blemmydes, *Epit. Phys.* cols. 1224C–1225 A (cap. 24.21). This philosophical principle found its way—via Hellenic paideia—also into the apocalyptic tradition, e. g., Rv 10:6, cf. Andreas Caesariensis, *In Apoc.* cap. 28 (p. 108) (comm. on Rv 10:6). Louth 2009, p. 215 aptly characterized Plato's *Timaeus* and the biblical *Genesis* as the "twin pillars" of patristic cosmology.

27 Alternatively, Magdalino 2003, pp. 239–240 proposed to distinguish three approaches that were used to estimate the date of the end: identifying apocalyptic signs ("blind dating"), calculating precise dates ("computus dating"), and following the chronology of the apocalyptic tradition ("dating on the side"). See also Brandes 2021a, pp. 288–289. In my view, the first and third categories are largely congruous, as signs of the end, e. g., catastrophic events, are constituent elements of the apocalyptic chronology. Conversely, a calamity could qualify only as a sign of the end if the apocalyptic chronology allowed for it. Thus, I treat the categories of "blind dating" and "dating on the side" as two instances of event-based prognostication.

https://doi.org/10.1515/9783112230114-003

vored the latter.[28] After all, specific catastrophic events—earthquakes, famines, and wars (Mt 24:7, Mk 13:8, Lk 21:11)—were indisputable harbingers of the end, while Scripture abounds in warnings against inquiring about the exact date of the end (Acts 1:7, cf. Mk 13:32, Mt 24:36, 1 Thes 5:1–2, Rv 16:15). This chapter discusses the prevalent views among the Eastern Romans pertaining to the anticipated lifespan of the world and, concomitantly, the expected timeframe of its dissolution. The Byzantines pursued two main strategies to date the *synteleia:* performing arithmetic computations and examining the signs of the end. Both strategies were informed by a general tendency to defer the end beyond one's own lifetime.

1.1 End-time computations

Notwithstanding the biblical admonitions, Byzantine visionaries repeatedly tried to work out the date of the *synteleia.* They supported their claims with various calculations. The most popular computational scheme was based on the presumption that protology foreshadows eschatology, i.e., that the creation of the world in seven days prefigures typologically the entire duration of world history. Biblical support for this view was found in Ps 89:4 (LXX) and 2 Pt 3:8, which stipulate that one day for God equals a thousand years for mankind. Accordingly, the seven days of creation would correspond to 7000 years. But strictly speaking, God created the world in six days (Gn 1:1–2:3), which meant that the world would not exceed 6000 years after its creation, which—according to the Alexandrian calendar—had taken place on 25 March 5493 BC.[29]

Accordingly, early Christians could expect the *synteleia* to transpire around the year 6000 AM (*anno mundi*), or c. 500 AD. Hippolytos of Rome (d. c. 235 AD) famously endorsed this calculation in his *Commentary on Daniel,* cautiously postponing the end by two and half centuries.[30] Curiously, once the year 500 AD had drawn near, expectations of an imminent end became scarce. A rare testimony

---

28 Magdalino 2000a, p. 27 and Magdalino 2008, pp. 125–126 noticed that the detection of apocalyptic signs (event-based) was given precedence over numerical calculations (date-based reckoning) in early Byzantium.

29 On the Alexandrian calendar, see Grumel 1958, pp. 85–97 and Mosshammer 2008, pp. 190–203. It was gradually replaced by the Byzantine calendar, which dated the creation of the world to 1 September 5509 before Christ. By the tenth century, the Byzantine calendar had become the standard. For details, see Grumel 1958, pp. 111–128 and Mosshammer 2008, pp. 278–316. The typology of the cosmic week is discussed by Daniélou 1948.

30 Hippolytus, *In Dan.* IV.23–24 (pp. 244–250).

can be found in the Greek redaction of the *Tiburtine Sibyl*, the so-called *Oracle of Baalbek*, which prognosticated that Constantinople would fall around 510 AD: "Do not boast, city of Byzantium, thou shalt not hold imperial sway for thrice sixty of thy years!"[31] The prediction signifies that the destruction of the imperial capital would be followed by the dissolution of the Christian Roman Empire and the arrival of the Antichrist, as recounted in detail in the Sibylline narrative. But the *Oracle of Baalbek* is a rare example. The apocalyptic silence from the early sixth century is conspicuous, especially if seen in the context of the tangible end-time trepidations during the mid-sixth century, which were fueled by earthquakes, warfare, and disease.[32] One wonders whether the year 500 really did not trigger much apocalyptic apprehension or whether the evidence has simply not reached us.[33]

The sources for end-time calculations are more plentiful for the period between 500 and 1000 AD. Prominent computational methods included exegetical arguments and numerical interpretations of symbolic letters and names (gematria). For instance, the *Hexaemeron*, commonly attributed to Anastasios of Sinai (d. after 700), advanced an exegetical argument based on Mt 25:6 and 1 Thes 5:2, showing that a literal reading of the Gospel verses places the arrival of the Messiah in the middle of the eighth century.[34] The two passages state that the Messiah would arrive at midnight, which corresponds to the first quarter of the Byzantine day. Given the above-mentioned equivalence of a day with a thousand years, the first quarter of the seventh day equates to the year 6250 AM, that is, to the mid-eighth century AD.[35] Alternatively, a contemporary of Anastasios, Theophanios the Monk, advanced a gematric calculation. Utilizing the numerical value of the name Ἰησοῦς, which totals 888, he predicted that the world would end in the year 6388 AM (880 AD). Advancing this calculation in c. 710 AD, Theophanios

---

31 *SibTibGr* ll. 94–95: μὴ καυχῶ, Βυζαντία πόλις, τρὶς γὰρ ἑξηκοστὸν τῶν ἐτῶν σου οὐ μὴ βασιλεύσεις. – Translation by Alexander 1967, p. 25. One arrives at 510 AD if one adds thrice sixty (180) years to 330 AD, the year Constantinople was consecrated.

32 On apocalypticism during Justinian's reign, see Rubin 1951, Scott 1985, pp. 107–109, Meier 2003, pp. 643–646, *passim*, and de Lange 2007, pp. 279–283.

33 Brandes 1997 collected indirect witnesses to apocalyptic sentiments around the year 500 and convincingly argued that some considered Emperor Anastasios (r. 491–518) the Antichrist, who was expected to usher in a reign of terror and trigger the *synteleia*. The Antichrist motif will be discussed in more detail in chapter 3.

34 Anastasius Sinaita, *Hex.* VII.2.1 (pp. 210). See further Magdalino 2000a, p. 28, Magdalino 2003, p. 246, and Magdalino 2008, p. 128.

35 The year 6250 AM corresponds to 741/742 AD according to the Byzantine calendar and to 757/758 AD according to the Alexandrian calendar. It is uncertain which calendar the author adopted.

effectively postponed the *eschaton* by 170 years.[36] Similarly, Patriarch Germanos I of Constantinople (715–730) professed that when the bishop blesses his congregation with his fingers forming the ligature stigma (͵ϛ) and phi (φ), he symbolically announces the year of Christ's Second Coming, i. e., the year 6500 AM (c. 1000 AD), which equals the sum of the two letters' gematric value.[37] Apparently, Germanos preferred the comfortable distance of a couple of centuries over the menacing proximity of a few decades. His preference echoes Hippolytos' and Theophanios' strategy to postpone the *synteleia* to the not-so-near future.[38]

Many Byzantines—not only Germanos I—favored the period around 1000 AD as a candidate date for the end, as it marked the midpoint of the seventh millennium (6500 AM) and the millenarian anniversary of Christ's incarnation and resurrection.[39] Another proponent was Nikētas David the Paphlagonian, who advanced a series of calculations seeking to substantiate the view that the world would reach its end a thousand years after the incarnation, i. e., around the year 6500 AM (991/992 AD).[40] Ihor Ševčenko and Paul Magdalino have published further evidence that testifies to the erstwhile popularity of this view.[41]

With the passage of the year 1000 AD, voices multiplied in refutation of that computation. A case in point is the *Dioptra of Philip the Monk*, which refuted the claim that the *eschaton* would transpire 6000 years after the creation. Such refutation was an easy task, given that the deadline had already lapsed by the time the *Dioptra* was written in the late eleventh century. For the same reason, the *Dioptra* rejected the millenarian reading of Rv 20:1–6, according to which the end times would materialize a thousand years after the incarnation (or resurrection). It ar-

36 Von Dobschütz 1903, pp. 550, 556. See further Magdalino 2003, p. 267.

37 Germanus, *Historia myst.* §33 (p. 82). The numeric value of stigma (preceded by a diacritical mark) is 6000, while phi signifies 500. The combined value amounts to 6500.

38 We know that Hippolytos' end-time calculation was still read in the eighth and ninth centuries, as testified by Patriarch Photios (d. c. 893), who reviewed and dismissed it out of hand on the basis that it had been falsified by the course of history. See Photius, *Bibl.* cod. 202 (III, pp. 101–102).

39 See Magdalino 2000a, pp. 29–30 and Magdalino 2003, who demonstrated that Byzantium saw an upsurge in millenarian anxieties around the year 1000. See further Cupane 2014, pp. 57–58, who has suggested that the significant increase of heavenly visions dating to the tenth century was due to millenarian expectations.

40 Nicetas David Paphlagonius, *Epist.* ll. 30–43 (pp. 192–193). See further Mango 1984, pp. 435–436, Paschalidēs 1999, pp. 235–238, Magdalino 2003, p. 269, and Brandes 2011, p. 314.

41 Ševčenko 2002 and Magdalino 2002.

gued instead that the timing of the end was contingent solely upon the heavenly ranks of the righteous souls reaching their full number, following Rv 14:1–5.[42]

Another interpretation is reported by John Tzetzēs, who—in the middle of the twelfth century—testified to anxieties that Constantinople would be destroyed prior to its millennial anniversary: "Woe to you, o Seven-Hilled City, for you shall not be a thousand years old."[43] Apparently, once the turn of the eleventh century had left millenarian expectations unfulfilled,[44] the notion of a thousand-year rule was transferred from the Roman Empire to Constantinople, the New Rome. This meant that the *synteleia* was yet again postponed to the not-so-near future, lying in the early fourteenth century if counting from the consecration of Constantinople in 330 AD.

Renewed apocalyptic expectations were voiced in the Palaiologan period. The *Prediction of Andritzopoulos* argued that the gematric value of the Greek word for cross (σταυρός), which amounts to 1271, was fulfilled during the reign of Michael VIII Palaiologos (r. 1259–1282).[45] Accordingly, the fulfillment of this symbolic number indicated the irreversible destruction of the Church and the Roman Empire' unleashing the Antichrist, who would trigger the Second Coming.[46] Finally, in the fifteenth century, the view that history would come to a close at the end of the seventh millennium, i.e., 1492 AD, gained the support of prominent church members, such as Archbishop Symeōn of Thessaloniki (d. 1429) and Patriarch Gennadios Scholarios (d. c. 1472).[47]

These and other computational predictions drew on the assumption that the (six or seven) days of creation prefigured the cosmic duration of the world.[48] It

---

42 Philippus Solitarius, *Diopt.* III.6 (pp. 142, l. 4–p. 144, l. 24), esp. p. 144, ll. 23–24: ὁπόταν τοίνυν πληρωθῇ ὁ ἀριθμὸς ἐκείνων [scil. τῶν ἁγίων καὶ δικαίων] ἐκδέχου τὴν συντέλειαν αἰῶνος τοῦ παρόντος. | Whenever, then, the number of those [i.e., saints and righteous ones] shall be made full, expect the consummation of the present age! – See further Podskalsky 1972, pp. 98–99.

43 Tzetzes, *Hist.* p. 370, l. 663 and Tzetzes, *Epist.* p. 88, l. 9 (*Epist.* 59): οὐαί σοι, ὦ ἑπτάλοφε, ὅτι οὐ χιλιάσεις. – See further Mango 1980, p. 212.

44 For apocalyptic expectations around the year 1000 AD in Byzantium, see Brandes 2000 and Brandes 2011, as well as Magdalino 2003 and Magdalino 2007b.

45 Two gematric computations are possible, yielding roughly the same outcome. The two possibilities depend on how one reads the first two letters (σ͟τ͟) in the word σταυρός: 1) as two letters: 2͟0͟0͟ + 3͟0͟0͟ + 1 + 400 + 100 + 70 + 200 = 1271 AD, or 2) as one letter: 6͟0͟0͟0͟ + 1 + 400 + 100 + 70 + 200 = 6771 AM (1262/3 AD).

46 *PraedAndritz* ll. 1–14.

47 See Turner 1964, pp. 369–371, Podskalsky 1974, p. 357, and especially Rigo 1992.

48 The Urzeit-Endzeit typology was not only used to determine the ultimate age of the world but also to estimate the duration of the destruction of the world. *VisEnoch* p. 386, ll. 6–8 describes how the earth would be destroyed by a seven-day-long global conflagration. Translation in Issaverdens 1901, pp. 322–323. The Armenian *Vision of Enoch the Just* goes back to a lost Greek

was commonly believed that somewhere between the sixth and seventh millennium the *eschaton* would occur, which largely coincided with the millennial timespan of the Byzantine Empire.[49] The various dates that visionaries and exegetes proposed repeatedly failed to materialize, so the New Testament injunction remained valid and the exact time of the end continued to be elusive. As the *absolute* date of the end proved unattainable, various attempts were made to establish its *relative* date. An authoritative and ostensibly reliable means to learn about the undisclosed timing of the *synteleia* was to study the signs of the end together with their chronological sequence.

1.2 Narrative sequence

Byzantine apocalyptic literature provided its audience with a rather coherent chronology of the end times. Part and parcel of this chronology were the motifs pertaining to natural catastrophes and moral decay derived from the canonical Scriptures. Natural calamities (Mt 24:7, Lk 21:11), moral decadence (Mt 24:12, 2 Tm 3:1–9), and the appearance of pseudo-prophets (Mt 24:11, Mk 13:22, Rv 19:20) were indisputable signs of the end.[50] The potent imagery of those signs was variously arranged in visionary accounts, and by the eighth century it had coalesced into a standard narrative of the future. This narrative was most frequently put forward in apocryphal prophecies attributed to the Church Father Methodios of Patara (d. 311), or the Prophet Daniel, or the Emperor Leo VI (d. 912). Although this narrative was continuously recombined, its central themes remained stable, persisting even to this day in circles that retain the Byzantine heritage.

The schematic narrative revolves around three major groups of protagonists: ideal-type emperors, the eschatological peoples (of the north and south),[51] and the Antichrist with the two (or three) witnesses. The narrative often begins with an initial period of hardship, usually suffered at the hands of an external enemy. The most pervasive external nemesis was the Arabs ("Ishmaelites"), who conquered and occupied vast swathes of Byzantine territory from the seventh century

Vorlage, which was probably composed in the early eighth century, as convincingly argued by Hultgård 1999.

49 See Brandes 2021a and Brandes 2021b for concise overviews of Byzantine end-time calculations.

50 Further references in Brandes 1997, p. 45.

51 The motif of the peoples of the south appears prominently in *VisEnoch* p. 378, ll. 10–11, p. 379, l. 14, p. 380, ll. 13, 23, *passim*. Translation in Issaverdens 1901, pp. 309, 310, 312, *passim*. It also appears in *ApcMeth I*, 10.6. The motif derives from Dn 11 and denotes the Arabs.

onwards. The Arab foe was expected to be vanquished by a divinely guided emperor, whose primary mission was to effect (I) the military defeat of all foreign enemies. Further eschatological tasks included (II) the inauguration of ultimate peace and prosperity and (III) a journey to Jerusalem, where the last emperor would abdicate his imperial dignity to Christ. It depended on the visionary's discretion to disclose whether this set of eschatological tasks would be accomplished by one or several rulers. While the *Apocalypse of Ps-Methodios* assigned them to a single emperor,[52] virtually all subsequent Medieval Greek apocalypses mentioned a sequence of emperors.[53] Among the various ideal-type monarchs tasked with eschatological duties, the Savior-Emperor or Warrior-Emperor received the greatest emphasis for his role in securing the military recovery (I).[54]

Adjacent to the Savior-Emperor, usually succeeding but at times also preceding him, is the arrival and defeat of the eschatological peoples of the north. This apocalyptic motif had evolved from the biblical figure of Gog and Magog (Ez 38–39, Rv 20:8). By the seventh century, it had become associated with Alexander the Great's northern peoples and identified with particular ethnic groups.[55] Thereupon, the identity of Gog and Magog was subject to various interpretations, ranging from the Huns and the Göktürks to the Rus' and the Bulgars.[56]

---

52 The Ps-Methodian motif of a Savior-Emperor markedly differs in its functions from previous descriptions of eschatological emperors, as they can be found, for instance, in the *SibTibGr* ll. 136–208. The debate whether this *topos* originated in Ps-Methodios (or in earlier, now lost, authors) does not need to detain us here. On this issue, see Alexander 1985, pp. 151–184, Möhring 2000, pp. 39–53, Greisiger 2014, pp. 172–180, Shoemaker 2018, pp. 64–89, Kraft 2019, pp. 533–540, and Brandes 2026.

53 See Wortley 1970a, p. 318 and Kraft 2012, pp. 242–243, 256. Given that Byzantine apocalypses tended to divide the initially unitary motif of the Ps-Methodian emperor, it is often more precise to speak of a series of last emperors rather than of *the* Last Emperor. Yet, it should be kept in mind that the *Apocalypse of Ps-Methodios*—and with it the unitary messianic motif—was continuously read, copied, and revised in Byzantium, as evidenced by the manuscript transmission, see Kraft 2018a, pp. 81–84. That is to say, the motif of the messianic emperor remained ambiguous throughout the centuries.

54 Brandes 1990 and Brandes 1991 coined the appellation "Savior-Emperor" (Retterkaiser), which I adopt here. The term well reflects the typological connection with Christ the Savior, which will be discussed below. Moreover, the term 'Savior-Emperor' is more appropriate than 'Last Emperor', given that this literary figure is usually not the very last emperor in the apocalyptic narrative. The position of ultimate ruler is usually reserved for the Antichrist. Alternatively, the term "Warrior-Emperor" was proposed by Wortley 1970b and Wortley 1977.

55 See Greisiger 2016. See further van Donzel and Schmidt 2010, pp. 15–32.

56 Jerome famously identified the Huns with the peoples enclosed by Alexander the Great in his *Epistula* 77, in Hieronymus, *Epist.* 77 §8 (pp. 45–46), while he identified the Scythians with the descendants of Gog in Hieronymus, *In Hiezech.* lib. 11 (p. 525, l. 1477) (comm. on Ez 38). See further, van Donzel and Schmidt 2010, p. 13 together with Greisiger 2016, pp. 65–66. Andrew of Caesarea

A characteristic element of Byzantine apocalypticism is the marked emphasis on the imperial capital. While some apocalypses foresee that Constantinople would be besieged and miraculously saved from conquest,[57] other texts focus on the City's final destruction at the *eschaton.*[58] After the Latin sack and occupation of Constantinople in 1204, Greek prophecies began to envision its reconquest and the reversal of imperial decline.[59] Thus, it has been rightly noted that historical apocalypses are, to a large extent, a Constantinopolitan genre, whose focus typically lies with the fate of the Queen of Cities.[60]

The final, climactic role in the schematic narrative was reserved for the Antichrist, whose origin, deeds, and eventual destruction was described in varying detail. As a rule of thumb: the later the prophecy, the shorter the descriptions of the Antichrist. In late Byzantine historical apocalypses, written after 1204, attention was primarily directed toward the political fortunes of the empire and its rulers.[61] Apparently, the waning of imperial power involved a lessened curiosity concerning the arrival of the Antichrist. This correlation needs to be seen against the commonly held belief that the Antichrist would rule as emperor and cause great havoc at the helm of the Roman polity.[62] Put differently, the decrease of imperial power minimized the unease and ambiguity concerning the emperors, who could be both saviors and oppressors.[63] The disambiguation of

---

testifies to the conflation of both interpretations, referring to "some who consider these to be the Scythians, the northmost peoples, whom we call the Huns [...]", see Andreas Caesariensis, *In Apoc.* cap. 63 (p. 223, ll. 8–9) (comm. on Rv 20:8): εἶναι δὲ ταῦτά τινες μὲν Σκυθικὰ ἔθνη νομίζουσιν ὑπερβόρεια, ἅπερ καλοῦμεν Οὐννικά [...] – Furthermore, Greisiger 2016, pp. 74–78 has argued that Gog and Magog were identified with the Göktürks during the reign of Herakleios. On the identification with the Rus', see Leo Diaconus, *Hist.* IX.6 (pp. 148–150). See further, Vasiliev 1946, pp. 166–168 and Brandes 1997, pp. 35–36. Cf. Hesychius, *Patr. Const.* II.47 (pp. 175–177). Concerning the possible identification with the Bulgars, see *UltVisDan I*, §§34–35 and its interpretation by Bousset 1899, p. 290.

57 *ApcMeth I*, 13.7–10 – *DiegDan* §§2.9–5.17.

58 *VisioDan* §4.21–23 – *ApcAndr* ll. 3989–99 – *UltVisDan I*, §§69–71.

59 *UltVisDan I*, §§41–48 – *VisDanSepCol I*, §§1.20–2.5 – *IntrpGenSch* ll. 23–33.

60 Dagron 1984, p. 328.

61 A good case in point is *VisDanSanHom.*

62 Hippolytus (Ps-), *De consum.* §20, ll. 2–4 – *ApcLeonConst* §16, ll. 430–435, §20, ll. 551–552 – *VaticBrys* ll. 6–8 – *VisDanSanHom* l. 731 – Oecumenius, *In Apoc.* cap. 9.13.8 (p. 224, ll. 290–294) – Andreas Caesariensis, *In Apoc.* cap. 36 (p. 137, ll. 9–16) (comm. on Rv 13:3), cap. 54 (p. 189, ll. 16–21) (comm. on Rv 17:11) – Arethas, *In Apoc.* cap. 30 (p. 343, ll. 8, 28), cap. 36 (p. 372, ll. 11–12). See further Alexander 1985, pp. 203–206.

63 The reduction of anxiety stands in contrast to developments in the Latin West, where the same ambiguity—associated with the papacy—intensified throughout the High Middle Ages due to the increase of papal power. See McGinn 1978.

the emperor—as only a sacred figure—is indicative of the erosion of his political influence. With the defeat of the Antichrist, the standard narrative of the future comes to an end. Historical apocalypses seldom go beyond this point.[64] Some sequential variations notwithstanding, Byzantine apocalypticism presented a schematic history of the future. A model of this schema is given on the next page in Table 1.[65]

Knowledge of this apocalyptic script conditioned the Byzantines' confidence that they lived close to the last days. Imperial ideology upheld that Byzantium was the last divinely ordained kingdom in history; it was the last of the four world empires known from Dn 2 and 7.[66] Medieval Greek apocalypses clearly endorsed that notion by placing the last emperors adjacent to the Antichrist. The exclusivity of the Christian Roman Empire must have evoked confidence if not pride. Moreover, the terror and horror of the anticipated calamities must have been reduced by the structured and hence predictable flow of events, which allowed the audience some amount of cognitive control.[67] Based on the standardized sequence of events, a perceptive Eastern Roman would have felt competent to discern how close the *synteleia* was and what to expect next. For instance, if there had not yet been an imperial abdication in Jerusalem, then the end was, arguably, not imminent. Similarly, if the peoples of the north had not been sighted yet, one could be confident in imploring God to delay the *synteleia* further.

1.3 Penitential deferral

Postponement is a key concern for apocalyptic traditions. It is a literary requirement as well as an institutional and psychological necessity. Apocalyptic literature requires constant postponement of the *eschaton* lest it renders itself invalid and void. The paradox of apocalypticism is that the apocalyptic worldview requires the delay of the desired consummation, as its realization would entail the annulment of the very worldview. Put differently, one either agrees that the world has come to an end and abandons the apocalyptic outlook, or maintains the apocalyp-

64 A notable exception is *ApcLeonConst* §§22–29.

65 For an alternative reconstruction of the narrative sequences of Greek and Syriac apocalypses, see Kraft 2012, pp. 245–249.

66 See Podskalsky 1972, pp. 4–64, Podskalsky 1984, pp. 440–443, Podskalsky 1986, and Dagron 1996, pp. 166–168. On the Greek origin of the universal history in Dn 2, see Momigliano 1982 and Kosmin 2018, pp. 142–148.

67 Cf. Alexander 1962, pp. 344–345.

Table 1: Narrative schema of historical apocalypses.

Source	Succession of literary motifs					
ApcMeth I	**A** (13.11 – 18)	**B** (13.19 – 21)	**C** (14.2 – 6)	/	**E** (14.1, 6 – 13)	**F** (14.14)
ApcAndr	**A** (ll.3824 – 58)	**C** (ll.3913 – 20)	**D** (ll.3989 – 99)	**B** (ll.4050 – 68)	**E** (ll.4069 – 91)	**F** (ll.4118 – 27)
ApcLeonConst	**B** (§14)	**A** (§15)	/	/	**E** (§§16 – 21)	**F** (§§22 – 29)
DiegDan	**A** (§§5.5 – 6.25)	/	/	**D** (§9.3 – 8)	**E** (§§11 – 14)	/
ExposDan I	**A** (p.674, l.13–p.675, l.24)	**B** (p.677, ll.5 – 20)	**D** (p.677, ll.20 – 23)	**C** (p.678, ll.1 – 6)	**E** (p.678, ll.7 – 11)	/
UltVisDan I	**B** (§§34 – 39)	**A** (§§47 – 59)	**C** (§§60 – 61)	**D** (§§69 – 71)	**E** (§§74 – 79)	**F** (§§83 – 85)
VisDanSepCol I	**A** (§2.5 – 21)	**C** (§2.22 – 29)	**B** (§2.30)	/	**E** (§2.32 – 33)	/

Abbreviations:
A motif: Savior-Emperor's victory and benefactions
B motif: arrival of the eschatological peoples
C motif: imperial abdication
D motif: destruction of Constantinople
E motif: arrival and deeds of the Antichrist
F motif: resurrection / last judgment

tic mindset but denies that the end has arrived.[68] Consequently, apocalyptic literature necessitates the assumption that the end is being postponed indefinitely. The contradictory relationship between the apocalyptic imagination and historical writing is encapsulated in the introductory remarks by Leo the Deacon (fl. late tenth century). His *History* begins with the assertion that numerous signs of the end had already been observed, "so that many people believe that life is now undergoing a transformation and that the expected Second Coming of the Savior and God *is drawing near, at the very gates*".[69] Leo the Deacon considered it likely that the *synteleia* was imminent, otherwise, he would not have reported this widespread belief. At the same time, he was well aware of the paradox implicit in writing a historical account: no one would be left to read it, if that belief turned out to be true.[70] Yet he still undertook the task with the supposition in mind that the *synteleia* may be further postponed.[71] The same rationale motivated the writing of apocalyptic prophecies.

The retardation of the end is not only a literary requirement but also an institutional necessity. Liturgical hymns and biblical commentaries—habitually composed by clergymen—persistently promote the view that the immorality in society continues to require penitence and the intercessory care of the Church. To protect their positions, Church officials have been naturally disposed to uphold the *status quo* and to seek the deferment of the end. After all, the Church ceases with the *eschaton*, as made utterly clear by the vision of a new heaven and earth in Rv 21:22. Thus, it is not surprising to find at the end of Romanos the Melodist's celebrated *Hymn on the Second Coming* a plea for a delayed end, beseeching Christ to grant time for repentance.[72] The same request was voiced a century later by Andrew of Caesarea in his *Commentary on Revelation.* Writing in the early seventh century, the bishop of Caesarea pleads "to be delivered from the trial of the prophesied [events] and to see neither the coming of the false Christ, nor

---

68 See Gutierrez 2005, pp. 54–55, who describes the paradox in reference to the more narrowly defined notion of millennialism.

69 Leo Diaconus, *Hist.* I.1 (p. 4, ll. 15–17): ὡς πολλοῖς δοκεῖν, ἀλλοίωσιν ἄρτι τὸν βίον λαβεῖν, καὶ τὴν προσδοκωμένην δευτέραν κατάβασιν τοῦ Σωτῆρος καὶ Θεοῦ *ἐπὶ θύραις ἐγγίζειν·* (Italics mine). – Translation by Talbot & Sullivan 2005, p. 56 (slightly changed). Cf. Mt 24:33, Mk 13:29: [...] ἐγγύς ἐστιν ἐπὶ θύραις.

70 Alternatively, Rubenstein 2019, p. 223 has suggested that some may have believed that their books would continue to exist in heaven. The mention of heavenly books in Rv 20:12 and *ApcAnast* §5 (p. 24) may speak in favor of such a view. However, one may object that those books are divine ledgers rather than man-made literary productions.

71 See further Mango 1980, p. 211, Ševčenko 2002, p. 572, and Magdalino 2003, pp. 242, 260–261.

72 Romanus Melodus, *Hymn.* 50, §24 (p. 266): [...] ἀλλά, σὲ καθικετεύω, δὸς καιρόν μοι μετανοίας, [...] – Translation by Lash 1995, p. 230: [...] But I implore you, give me time for repentance, [...].

the movement of the aforementioned nations, nor any death-bringing danger that compels us to apostatize from the saving faith".[73] The institutional survival of the Church depended on the postponement of the end. Crucially, the timing of the *eschaton* was indeterminate and perceived as open to change.

The deferral of the end was also a psychological need. The desire to delay the end of the world is a predictable reaction to the anticipated horrors of global destruction and ultimate punishment. A typical and traditional way to postpone the end was to assert that the heavenly vacancies needed to be filled first. Only if the heavenly ranks, which had become vacant by the devil's primordial rebellion, had been replenished, could the *eschaton* transpire.[74] This belief implies that if the death of a saint is postponed, the heavenly ranks remain incomplete and the end is deferred. It is this context in which one ought to read stories that describe the deferred death of a holy man. A case in point is a story in the *Life of Theodōros of Sykeōn*, which recounts how Saint Theodōros (d. 613) fell seriously ill and was approaching death. He adroitly convinced the angelic doctors who were verifying his moribund condition to intervene on his behalf and to have his lifetime extended so that he may have more time to repent his sins. If his request were to be granted, the saint emphasized, the credit for his repentance as well as for his future charitable deeds would go to his angelic intercessors.[75] Theodōros was a master of persuasion. He not only swayed the emperor and the patriarch to release him from his duty as Bishop of Anastasiopolis,[76] but he also convinced the angelic deputies to do his biddings. The cardinal idea behind this episode is that the timing of one's death was negotiable and that a crucial argument in any such negotiation was cumulative moral betterment. At the same time, it implies that the

---

73 Andreas Caesariensis, *In Apoc.* cap. 63 (p. 226): [...] τῆς τῶν προφητευθέντων πείρας ῥυσθῆναι καὶ μηδὲ τὴν τοῦ ψευδοχρίστου θεάσασθαι ἔλευσιν, μήτε τῶν προλεχθέντων ἐθνῶν τὴν κίνησιν μήτε κίνδυνον θανατηφόρον τῆς σωτηρίου πίστεως ἀποστῆναι βιαζόμενον, [...] – Cited by Magdalino 1993, p. 10 and Magdalino 2003, p. 266.

74 See Anastasius Sinaita, *Quaest.* 94 (pp. 149–150) – Philippus Solitarius, *Diopt.* III.6 (p. 144) – Symeon Neotheologus, *Orat.* I.8 (pp. 240–246). See further Magdalino 2003, p. 258 and Magdalino 2008, p. 130.

75 Georgius Eleusius, *VitTheoSyc* §39 (p. 35): Εἶπεν δὲ αὐτοῖς· 'ἐὰν τοῦτο ποιήσητε καὶ ἐμοὶ τὰ μεγάλα παρέχητε καιρὸν μετανοίας μοι ἐξαιτούμενοι, καὶ τῆς ἀπὸ τοῦ νῦν ἐργασίας μου καὶ μετανοίας τὸν μισθὸν κερδανεῖτε.' – Translation by Dawes and Baynes 1948, p. 116 (modified): He (scil. Theodōros) told them: 'If you do this and grant me the great service to request for me time for repentance, you will gain the reward for the repentance and my work from now on.' – On this text, see Kazhdan 1999, p. 23 and the references provided therein.

76 Georgius Eleusius, *VitTheoSyc* §79 (pp. 66–67).

blessed (μακάριος) Theodōros would not yet contribute to the replenishment of the heavenly ranks, which involves a delay of the *synteleia*.

Negotiation applied not only to the date of one's death but also to other spheres of eschatology. The Middle Byzantine *Apocalypse of the Virgin* offers a paramount example. In this moral apocalypse the Virgin launches repeated attempts at prompting Christ to show clemency for the souls that are tortured in the pre-resurrection afterlife. The Byzantine conception of the afterlife revolved around the notion of an interim state between death and the general resurrection, in which the souls of the deceased undergo preliminary judgment.[77] The souls of the righteous receive temporary bliss, while those of the wicked are exposed to preliminary yet gruesome tortures as a means of divine retribution. The *Apocalypse of the Virgin* describes the Theotokos' persistent labors to invoke Christ's mercy. Eventually, she succeeds in soliciting temporary relief from punishment.[78]

Similarly, historical apocalypses advance pleas and prayers that demonstrate how to placate divine wrath. For instance, the ninth-century *Vision of Daniel on the Last Times* puts an entreaty into the mouth of a Constantinopolitan crowd. The plea is promptly answered by granting temporary alleviation from afflictions.[79] Several other Byzantine apocalyptica reiterate the notion that pleas for divine clemency are not ineffective but, to the contrary, swiftly and graciously responded to.[80] Thus, the eschatological hardships—called "birth pangs" (ἀρχὴ ὠδίνων) based on Mt 24:8—could be negotiated and modified. Indeed, divine benevolence and omnipotence render it not only possible but also probable that the history of the future is updated for the benefit of those who repent.[81]

---

77 On the post-mortem fate of the soul, see Constas 2001, Baun 2007, pp. 300–312, and Marinis 2017, pp. 28–48.

78 *ApcMarVir* §29 (p. 126).

79 *VisioDan* §4.17–19: μὴ καταποντίσῃ ἡμᾶς ἡ ὀργή σου, κύριε, ἕως τέλος, ὅτι ἐκύκλωσεν ἡμᾶς ἐσχάτη ἄβυσσος τῶν ἁμαρτιῶν [ἡμῶν]. σῶσον τὸν λαόν σου, ὁ θεὸς ἡμῶν. καὶ σπλαγχνισθεὶς ὁ κύριος ἐπὶ τοῖς δάκρυσιν αὐτῶν ἐρεῖ τῷ ἀγγέλῳ· ἆρον τὴν ὀδύνην [ἀπὸ] τῆς γῆς ἕως καιρῶν τινων. | 'May Your wrath not drown us completely, Lord, since the final abyss of [our] sins has encircled us. Save Your people, our God!' And the Lord, feeling compassion upon their tears, will say to the angel: 'Take away the pain from the earth for some time.'

80 *AnonymVatic* p. 49, ll. 17–18: καὶ εἰσελεύσεται ἡ προσευχὴ αὐτοῦ [scil. τοῦ βασιλέως] εἰς τὰ ὦτα Κυρίου Σαβαώθ, [...] | And his [i.e., the emperor's] prayer will enter the ears of the Lord Sabaoth [...] – *NarrMend* ll. 46–47: καὶ τότε εἰσακούσεται κ(ύριο)ς τῆς δεήσεως αὐτῶν· καὶ θήσει τὰ ὦτα ἐπὶ τοὺς κατοικοῦντας τὴν γῆν· Translation in Brokkaar et al. 2002, p. 93 (modified): And then the Lord will yield to their prayer and will turn His ears to those who inhabit the earth. – *ApcMeth IV*, 13.11: καὶ ἐπακούσεται κύριος ὁ θεὸς τὰς φωνὰς καὶ τῶν κλαυθμῶν αὐτῶν. | And the Lord God will give ear to the sound of their laments.

81 John Chrysostom made this point explicit by highlighting the utility of genuine prophecy-making in inducing people to undergo a "change of heart" (μεταβολήν), which then prevents

The Byzantines' readiness to modify or altogether rewrite prophecies is well testified by the copious manuscript tradition. The late seventh-century *Apocalypse of Ps-Methodios* comes down in four Greek redactions in more than 40 manuscript copies,[82] the mid-tenth-century *Apocalypse of Andrew the Fool* was copied even more often, with about 80 codices containing redacted excerpts,[83] and the thirteenth-century *Last Vision of Daniel* was revised twice and copied at least 43 times.[84] Byzantine apocalyptica were continuously redacted, interpolated, and recontextualized. Not only the texts but also their conceptual building blocks underwent development. The *topos* of the Savior-Emperor, for instance, was reduplicated (or fragmented) into a series of monarchs who successively carry out the eschatological tasks stipulated by Ps-Methodios.[85] The open textuality is a manifest testimony to the belief that the *eschaton* could be changed and delayed. In fact, apocalyptic narratives had to defer the end, as it continuously failed to arrive. Thus, the generic requirement of apocalyptic literature to delay the *synteleia* coincided with the empirical fact that the end was continually delayed. In short, Medieval Greek apocalyptica share a common tendency of retardation and procrastination, which is typified by the protraction of the narrative and the postponement beyond the current generation.[86] The task of the chroniclers of the future was therefore to revise repeatedly the apocalyptic script, accounting for recent developments while renewing pleas for intercession and deferment.

---

ominous prophecies from coming true. Ioannis Chrysostomus, *Comm. in Jerem.* col. 741B–C (*prologus*), drawing on Jer 18:7–8. The passage has been translated and discussed by Magdalino 2019, pp. 185–186, 201–202.

82 The four redactions have been edited by Lolos 1976 and Lolos 1978. The second through fourth redactions have been largely ignored in scholarship. Attention has been restricted to the first redaction, which is a direct translation from Syriac. For a preliminary conspectus of the manuscript transmission, see Kraft 2018a, pp. 81–84.

83 The *Vita S. Andreae Sali* is contained—in whole or in part—in at least 120 Greek codices, of which about 80 copies contain the apocalyptic section—with or without the rest of the *Vita*. For an overview of the known manuscript transmission, see Rydén 1995, I, pp. 151–181 and Kraft 2018a, pp. 97–100.

84 See Kraft 2018a, pp. 115–116 and Kraft 2022, pp. 349–350, where 39 copies are identified. To those four further manuscripts should be added; one from Bucharest (cod. Bucurestiensis gr. 1087, fol. 9r–v, saec. XIX) and three from Mt Athos (cod. Megistēs Lavras M 68 (Eustratiadēs 1759), pp. 204–206, ann. 1772; cod. Panteleimonos 204 (Lambros 5711), pp. 713–715, saec. XIX; cod. Vatopediou 989, fols 65r–67v, saec. XIX).

85 See Brandes 1991, p. 35 and Kraft 2012, p. 252. Other *topoi* underwent reduplication as well. For instance, the figure of the Antichrist was duplicated in *ApcMeth IV*, 13.25–28 (discussed below). It is noteworthy that the different messianic tasks tended to be reassigned to a single monarch in the post-Byzantine period, e.g., *VatResCon I* §§3–4.

86 See Magdalino 2008, p. 126.

2 Velocity

> [...] un récit peut se passer d'anachronies,
> il ne peut aller sans *anisochronies*, ou, si l'on préfère
> (comme c'est probable), sans effets de *rythme*.[87]
> Gérard Genette

Byzantine historical prophecies present eschatological time as an orderly sequenced flow of events. Yet, upon close inspection, the diachronic timeline is marked by natural and phenomenological distortions. The *eschaton* was expected to produce objective distortions of time, with the natural duration of days and hours being suspended. In addition, Byzantine apocalyptica manipulate the subjective perception of eschatological time by literary means. They use irregular narrative speeds that depict eschatological time as unpredictable and disordered, while the textual transmission tends to postpone the *eschaton* to the indefinite future. This chapter examines the fabric of eschatological time from three related perspectives: the motifs embedded inside the texts, the narrative pacing throughout the texts, and the transmission history of the texts. These perspectives cover the literary motif of the shortening of days, the compositional technique of narrative speed, and the evolution of the text tradition.

2.1 Shortening of days

The course of history is depicted as a succession of homogeneous years in Byzantine apocalyptica. The duration of future years, months, and days is as uniform as that of traditional units of timekeeping. There is, however, one exceptional occurrence that upsets the objective uniformity: the phenomenon of the "shortening of days". This occurrence is described in the Gospel accounts of Mt 24:22 and Mk 13:20, where Christ predicts that the last days will be shortened so that the elect can better endure the ultimate afflictions.[88] The shortening of days is invoked in many Byzantine apocalypses, including the early sixth-century *Oracle of Baalbek*, the thirteenth-century *Last Vision of Daniel*, and the *Apocalypse of Leo of Con-*

87 Genette 1972, p. 123.

88 Mt 24:22: καὶ εἰ μὴ ἐκολοβώθησαν αἱ ἡμέραι ἐκεῖναι, οὐκ ἂν ἐσώθη πᾶσα σάρξ· διὰ δὲ τοὺς ἐκλεκτοὺς κολοβωθήσονται αἱ ἡμέραι ἐκεῖναι. | And except those days should be shortened, there should no flesh be saved: but for the elect's sake those days shall be shortened. – Translations of the Bible follow the King James version, unless stated otherwise. Cf. Mk 13:20 and *Barn. Epist.* 4:3. The motif is discussed by Bousset 1895, pp. 143–144 and Alexander 1985, pp. 209–211.

https://doi.org/10.1515/9783112230114-004

stantinople, whose current form was likely produced in the thirteenth century as well.[89] The motif also appears in Jewish, Zoroastrian, and Islamic apocalyptic traditions.[90]

Several Byzantine end-time narratives reaffirm the philanthropic purpose of the shortening of days, specifying that the days are shortened for the benefit of mankind.[91] There is no indication either in Byzantine apocalyptica or in the commentary tradition that the shortening of days was explained in cosmological terms, although such an explanation would have been easy to arrive at. A cosmological account could have, for instance, juxtaposed the potent imagery of the "rolling up of the heavens" in Rv 6:14 and the classical philosophical heritage that associated time and time keeping with the movement of the celestial spheres. Accordingly, it could have been reasoned that if the heavens were to disintegrate, time would have to change concomitantly. Yet, there is no evidence for such an explanation. The authoritative commentary on *Revelation* by Andrew of Caesarea (d. 614) does not give any cosmological significance to either the "rolling up of the heaven" or the "shortening of days".[92] In stark contrast, the Neoplatonist philosopher Simplikios (fl. 530s) presupposed a correlation between the alleged end of the world and the unraveling of time. In a well-known polemical passage, he confronts his Christian opponent Philoponos by arguing that the world was not going to end any time soon, given that there was no sign that the duration of days or hours were undergoing change.[93] The apocalyptic tradition, however,

89 *SibTibGr* ll. 178–180 – *UltVisDan I*, §79 – *ApcLeonConst* §21, ll. 562–567. The motif also appears in *SepVisDan* p. 131, ll. 6–7 – *ApcIoh* §8 (p. 76) – Hippolytus (Ps-), *De consum.* §35 – Philippus Solitarius, *Diopt.* III.6 (p. 150, ll. 27–31). Cf. *OracLeon* p. 66, l. 4 (Orac. 5), which uses a metaphorical expression, talking about a miscarriage of temporal movement (χρόνων κίνησις ἐξημβλωμένη). This potent image combines the simile of the "birth pangs" (Mt 24:8) with the expectation of temporal anomalies at the *eschaton*. A more general notion of God shortening time at the *eschaton* appears in *VisNiph* §83 (p. 209).

90 Dimant 2001, pp. 37–38 (*4Q385*, frag. 4), Stone and Henze 2013, pp. 25, 26, 36 (*4 Ezra* 4:26, 4:34, 6:21), pp. 94, 119, 138 (*2 Baruch* 20:1, 54:1, 83:1), Ben-Sasson 2022, p. 361 (Hebrew *Vision of Daniel* from the St. Petersburg collection), Cereti 1995, p. 154 (*Zand ī Wahman Yasn*), and Cook 2017, p. 345 (*Kitāb al-fitan*, no. 1517). See further Reeves 1994, pp. 265–267, Hultgård 1998, p. 75, Cook 2002, p. 15, and Ben-Sasson 2026, pp. 154–156.

91 *UltVisDan I*, §79 – Philippus Solitarius, *Diopt.* III.6 (p. 150, ll. 27–31).

92 Andreas Caesariensis, *In Apoc.* cap. 18 (pp. 70–71) (comm. on Rv 6:14), cap. 26 (p. 97, ll. 17–20) (comm. on Rv 9:5). Cf. Oecumenius, *In Apoc.* cap. 4.15.6 (p. 130, ll. 332–336), cap. 5.19.3 (p. 148, l. 334). Similarly, Arethas, *In Apoc.* cap. 18 (pp. 279–280), cap. 30 (p. 339, ll. 30–32).

93 Simplicius, *In Arist. Phys.* VIII.10 (p. 1335, ll. 5–11): ὁ τοίνυν οὐρανὸς πρὸ ἑξακισχιλίων καὶ πρὸς ἐνιαυτῶν, ὡς οὗτος οἴεται, γεγονὼς καὶ ἐπ' ἐσχάτοις ὢν ἤδη τῶν ἡμερῶν, ὡς καὶ τοῦτο πάντως αὐτὸν ἀρέσκει, πῶς οὐδὲν παρακμαστικὸν καὶ πρὸς φθορὰν ὁδεῦον ἡμῖν ἐνεδείξατο; καίτοι κἂν μηδὲν ἄλλο, πάντως γε κατὰ τὴν κίνησιν ἀργότερος ὤφελε νοεῖσθαι κατὰ τὸ ἔσχατον γῆρας

did not adopt such scientific rationale and retained the moralizing justification offered in the Bible.[94]

The observation that the apocalyptic tradition in Byzantium stood clear of scientific approaches is reinforced by the fact that the shortening of days implies chronometric fluctuations. If a year is shortened into a month, time is compressed by the factor of 12, while if a month is shortened into a week, the factor of 4 is applied, and so on. There are no regular acceleration rates in the series of the shortening of days. The acceleration is, mathematically speaking, inconsistent. Apparently, numerical consistency was not a concern for apocalyptists. Instead, they prioritized literary consistency, signifying lexical stability when transitioning one temporal unit into another. In brief, the shortening of days is a temporal anomaly that is solely explained in ethical terms, not in cosmological or mathematical ones.

The motif is based on the presumption that suffering causes the perception of time to slow down. To ease suffering, time needs to speed up. There is ample evidence that the Byzantines perceived time as decelerating in moments of hardship. A good witness is John Kaminiatēs, who experienced "the stretching of time" (τοῦ καιροῦ τὴν ἐπίτασιν) amidst the horrors of carnage, thirst, and fear during sack of Thessaloniki in 904.[95] Conversely, the contraction of time was understood to diminish suffering and, hence, to serve as a philanthropic act of relief. Given that the greatest hardships were expected to occur during the Antichrist's reign, the shortening of days was most commonly applied to the three-and-a-half-year rule of the Antichrist. The *Apocryphal Apocalypse of John*, the *Last Vision of Daniel*, and the *Apocalypse of Leo of Constantinople* all reiterate this interpretation, which traces back to the Hippolytan tradition.[96]

τυγχάνων. καίτοι οὔτε τὰς ἡμέρας οὔτε τὰς νύκτας οὔτε τὰς ὥρας μακροτέρας ποιεῖ νῦν [...] | That man [i.e., Philoponos] thinks that the heaven came to be over six thousand years ago and he is certainly pleased to suppose that it is now in its last days. How is it, then, that it has given us no indication that it is past its prime and heading towards its end? In fact, even if nothing else, we should certainly notice at least that it is moving slower if it is reaching the extremity of old age. But as things are, it is not making the days or nights or hours any longer now. – Translation by McKirahan 2001, p. 121.

94 The moralizing explanation was endorsed also by the Church Fathers and became the standard. For references, see Tamiōlakēs 2011, pp. 271–272. See further Agamben 2001, p. 99, who argues that (Western) Christianity dissociates time from the physical motion of the stars and considers it—following Augustine—a purely psychological phenomenon. It remains to be examined to what extent this observation applies to Eastern Orthodoxy. For an insightful contrast between the Augustinian (psychological) and Plotinian (metaphysical) notions of time, see Callahan 1948, pp. 88–187, 196–204.

95 Ioannis Caminiatae, *De expug.* §57 (p. 49, l. 91).

96 *ApcIoh* §8 (p. 76) – *UltVisDan I*, §§78–79 – *ApcLeonConst* §21, ll. 562–567. Cf. Hippolytus, *De Christ. et Antichrist.* §62 – Hippolytus (Ps-), *De consum.* §33, ll. 5–6 and §35, ll. 1–6.

The *Apocalypse of Leo of Constantinople* applies the motif of the shortening of days not only to the reign of the Antichrist but also to a new narrative episode. Following the destruction of the Antichrist, the phenomenon of accelerated time is applied to a newborn scion of the imperial family. The text reads:

> After he [i.e., the Antichrist] is carried off into the fire, a child will be born in the imperial chambers at the first hour of the night, and at the fourth hour he will speak, and at the seventh hour he will grow his first beard, and in the second hour of the day he will seek a woman in marriage. [...] And straightway at that evening there will be a great and fearful bang in the heaven [...] and from that fear all will die and lie asleep for three hours.[97]

The grotesque image of a newborn growing a beard and looking for a wife within hours of birth fleshes out the biblical motif and raises the expectation that not only outside events but also human nature itself will be subject to temporal hastening. The passage raises the expectation that the contraction of natural time is not a mere corollary of the Antichrist's reign but a persistent condition of the end times, which reshapes the very nature of the last newborn in the imperial chambers, the last porphyrogennetos.[98] The lifetime of the post-Antichrist ruler is cut radically short; he lives less than a day. Born at night, he grows up at day and perishes in the evening. The ominous and monstrous occurrence of such a super-accelerated aging precedes a cosmic bang that kills all mankind and sets the stage for the general resurrection, which is said to occur virtually instantaneously, within three hours. The apocalyptic "big bang" (μέγας κτύπος) in the *Apocalypse of Leo of Constantinople* heralds the end of history. It is directly followed by the angelic trumpets that inaugurate the resurrection.[99] The shortening of man's lifespan functions as the transition point from this-worldly to otherworldly time, from the structured temporal progression of cosmic life to the atemporal stagnation of the afterlife. In conclusion, the shortening of days describes an *objective* alteration of temporality, in which the natural passage of time unravels through acceleration, marking an infallible sign of the end.

---

97 *ApcLeonConst* §22, ll. 588–598: Μετὰ δὲ τὸ ἀπενεχθῆναι αὐτὸν εἰς τὸ πῦρ, γεννηθήσεται παιδίον ἐν τοῖς οἴκοις τῶν βασιλέων ὥρᾳ πρώτῃ τῆς νυκτός, καὶ ὥρᾳ τετάρτῃ λαλήσει, καὶ ὥρᾳ ἑβδόμῃ γενήσεται ἀρχηγένειος, καὶ ὥρᾳ δευτέρᾳ τῆς ἡμέρας ζητήσει λαβεῖν γυναῖκα· [...] εὐθέως δὲ τὸ δειλινὸν ἐκεῖνο γενήσεται κτύπος μέγας καὶ φοβερὸς ἐν τῷ οὐρανῷ [...] καὶ ἀπὸ τοῦ φόβου ἐκείνου πάντες ἀποθανοῦνται καὶ ἀφυπνώσουσιν ἕως ὥρας τρεῖς. – Cf. *4 Ezra* 6:21.

98 The notion that there will be another Constantinopolitan ruler after the Antichrist is a unique addition to the apocalyptic script. It is based on the compositional technique to reduplicate characters along typological lines, which will be discussed in chapter 3.

99 *ApcLeonConst* §22, ll. 599–605.

2.2 Narrative speed

Medieval Greek apocalypses also convey *subjective* alterations in the flow of time. The rhythm and speed of those texts are not monotonous and unchanging. To the contrary, they are decidedly anisochronous, that is, they are characterized by fluctuating speeds.[100] Apocalypses narrate events and characters with varying degrees of detail. A detail-rich account not only emphasizes the significance of the character or event but also slows down the narrative. The more detailed a particular section, the slower the overall narrative proceeds. Conversely, the fewer details provided, the quicker events appear to pass. The perception of time that a narrative creates depends on the relationship between the narrated time—the duration of an event within the narrative—and the narrating time—the duration it takes the narrator to recount the event. The ratio of those two factors establishes the narrative speed. Alternatively, this ratio can also be called narrative velocity. Velocity is generally defined as the distance moved during a constant unit of time in a particular direction. Applying this definition to our investigation means that velocity is the ratio between narrated time (moved distance) and narrating time (constant unit of time) in the direction towards the *eschaton.* In the context of apocalyptic narratives, the terms narrative speed and velocity can be used interchangeably, as all apocalypses share one (and the same) direction.

The narrative speed (or velocity) accelerates when events are presented in summary and decelerates when events are depicted in a scenic way.[101] Direct speech, for instance, is a scenic device that approximates the duration of the event to the actual narrating time and thus temporarily slows down the narrative speed. Byzantine apocalyptica present the reader with many direct speeches, such as divine commands and prayers.[102] The general mode of presentation, however, is summaries. The narrative speeds of summaries can differ significantly. For instance, in the mid-tenth century *Apocalypse of Andrew the Fool* the narrator prophesies the deeds of a series of eschatological rulers, for whom we are given the anticipated lengths of their reigns.[103] Each reign is described in varying

100 Genette 1972, p. 123 pointed out that virtually every narrative contains anisochronies (i.e., changes in the temporal rhythm), either through acceleration or deceleration.

101 See Genette 1972, pp. 122–144, Prince 1982, pp. 54–59, and de Jong and Nünlist 2007a, pp. 10–12.

102 Direct speech appears frequently in historical apocalypses but is most prominent in moral apocalypses, following the model of *Revelation.*

103 On the mid-tenth-century dating, see Rydén 1978, p. 155, Rydén 1995, I, p. 41, Magdalino 1999, p. 86, and Kazhdan 2006, pp. 193–194. Parts of the apocalyptic section may have originated earlier. See Greisiger 2017, pp. 89–94, who has argued that the vigorous rejection of eschatological

detail. If we quantify the narrating time with the word count of the respective passage and divide it by the narrated time, we can establish a ratio that indicates the respective narrative speed. The lower the ratio, the higher the speed. By comparing the different narrative speeds one can establish the rhythm of the prophecy.

The basis of the following computation is the critical edition by Lennart Rydén.[104] It needs to be remembered that a critical edition is a hypothetical reconstruction of a lost original, based on a collation of different text witnesses. Consequently, the word count should be considered only an estimate, as it can differ from manuscript to manuscript. Slight variations in the word count do occur but are negligible, as they do not affect the overall impression of how fast or slow the narrative proceeds. That is to say, the established ratio is indicative of the rhythm, but it is not an absolute value. The critical edition of the *Apocalypse of Andrew the Fool* supplies the following numerical figures (Table 2):

Table 2: Narrative speed in the *Apocalypse of Andrew the Fool.*

Reference	Motif	Narrated time	Word count	Ratio
ll. 3824–3858	a savior-emperor rules	32 years	364	11.4
ll. 3859–3884	a son of lawlessness rules	3 ½ years	268	76.6
ll. 3885–3906	a pagan emperor rules	unspecified	217	N/A
ll. 3907–3912	an Ethiopian emperor rules	12 years	61	5.1
ll. 3913–3920	an Arabian emperor rules and abdicates	1 year	82	82
ll. 3921–3923	three young men reign in peace	150 days	20	48.8
ll. 3923–3959	civil war among the three men	unspecified	362	N/A
ll. 3960–3988	a wicked woman rules	unspecified	312	N/A

The *Apocalypse of Andrew the Fool* begins with a sequence of good and bad Constantinopolitan rulers. The sequence consists of five monarchs, who are followed by a triumvirate (sixth figure) and a wicked woman (seventh figure). The five-plus-two theme resembles the seven-kings motif from Rv 17:9–10, which likely informed this elaborate chronology of eschatological rulers.[105] The sequence is

inclusivism, i.e., the view that the Jews have a positive role to play in Christian eschatology, may date back to the early seventh century.

104 Rydén 1995.

105 See Wortley 1973, pp. 252–253 and Kraft 2012, p. 243. The *Apocalypse of Andrew the Fool* uses also other material from *Revelation.* Notable parallels include *ApcAndr* ll. 3995–99, cf. Rv 18:21

marked by an irregular narrative speed that oscillates between acceleration and deceleration.

One might doubt whether those shifts are of any importance, given that the narrated time frames comprise apocalyptically connoted numbers: 32, 12, 3 ½. Those numbers are *topoi*. This observation, however, does not affect the validity, historicity, or phenomenological impact of a motif, such as a time period. *Topoi* are rhetorical devices that contextualize events and characters, which can be fictional, but they can just as well be reflective of historical facts.[106] Moreover, the metatextual impact that a narrative has on its audience is not affected by issues of historicity. Even an ahistorical, allegorical interpretation would have to account for the fluctuations in the narrative speed. That is to say, the topical durations ought to be taken seriously—if not literally—just as any unbiased Byzantine reader would have done.

Another example is the *Apocalypse of Ps-Methodios*. This work is a world chronicle that starts with Adam and Eve in Paradise and closes with the Second Coming. It traverses seven millennia of world history and highlights the period that directly precedes the *eschaton*. Accordingly, it consists of two sections: a historical (*ApcMeth I*, 1–13.6) and a prophetic (*ApcMeth I*, 13.7–14.14) part. It was composed in Syriac during the late seventh century and translated into Greek by the early eighth century. By and large, the Greek translation follows closely the Syriac *Vorlage*.[107] Thus, the examination of the narrative speed in the Syriac original and the Greek translation should yield roughly the same results. For the sake of conciseness, the following analysis is restricted to the Greek textual tradition.

The *Apocalypse of Ps-Methodios* saw repeated reworkings in Byzantium, resulting in four Greek redactions. Each redaction contains the prophetic part with its emphasis on the deliverance from the Arabs through a divinely appointed Christian emperor. It appears that successive generations viewed the message of messianic deliverance as the nucleus of the *Apocalypse of Ps-Methodios*. The over-

(the destruction of Constantinople), *ApcAndr* ll. 4075–76, cf. Rv 20:8, 2 Jn 1:7 (the deceptive nature of the Antichrist), and *ApcAndr* ll. 4111–13, cf. Rv 9:4, 9:10 (the plague of demonic creatures).

106 See Delouis 2003, p. 240, Pratsch 2005, pp. 364–371, and Baun 2007, pp. 135, 247, who hold that a *topos* does not necessarily invalidate the historicity of a given passage, while Magdalino 1983, pp. 328–329 points out that *topoi* served to add emphasis and convey a sense of order and security by repeating commonplaces. See also Cherchi 1976.

107 For comparison of the Syriac and Greek versions, see Alexander 1985, pp. 52–60, Aerts and Kortekaas 1998, I, pp. 7–18, Kraft 2012, pp. 224–226, and Bonura 2025, pp. 165–170. The most significant additions to the Greek translation are a paraphrase of (Ps-)Anastasios of Sinai's *Disputation against the Jews* (*ApcMeth I*, 10.4), the description of an Arab assault on Constantinople (*ApcMeth I*, 13.7–10), and the inclusion of the two witnesses Enoch and Elijah (*ApcMeth I*, 14.11–12, cf. Rv 11:1–14). Those additions only slightly retard the narrating time.

all tendency of the reworkings was to shorten the narrative and to focus on this nucleus.

The second and third redactions abridged the narrative by roughly one-third, while the fourth redaction compressed the text by an additional third. Notwithstanding the omissions, the narrative speed does not change substantially in the second and third redactions. Significant changes occur only in the contents and structure of the narrative. The most noteworthy change is the rearrangement of the chapters four through nine in the third redaction, with the result that the transition from one millennium to the next is not as clearly demarcated as in the first two redactions.[108] Furthermore, the third Greek redaction reassigns chapter four to the sixth millennium, instead of the original fourth millennium, which the third redaction omits altogether.[109]

The fourth redaction introduces the most substantial changes, as it is the shortest of all. It omits the vast majority of the historical part and begins *in media res* with the Arab conquests (*ApcMeth IV*, 10.6). While it retains the main elements of the prophetic section, it introduces a few notable changes. It interpolates an emotional plea for divine assistance (*ApcMeth IV*, 13.11) and adds a diabolic ruler-figure to the very end of the narrative (*ApcMeth IV*, 13.25–28). This satanic king is difficult to distinguish from the Antichrist, who is omitted from the text. For our purposes, the most remarkable novelty is the omission of any timescale. The reader is left in the dark as to when and for how long the described events are supposed to take place. Consequently, the narrative speed cannot be established for the last reworking of the *Apocalypse of Ps-Methodios*. Anastasios Lolos' edition provides the basis for the following tables (Table 3), which establish the narrative speeds for every redaction except the fourth one.[110]

---

108 For a convenient overview of the chronology of the *Apocalypse of Ps-Methodios*, see Garstad 2012, pp. xvi–xviii. It is noteworthy that the edition of the third redaction published by Lolos 1978 —and prior to him by Istrin 1897, II, pp. 51–66—is based on a single Athonite manuscript: cod. Panteleimonos 789 (Lambros 6296), saec. XVIII. On this manuscript, see Lambros 1900, pp. 433–434. Other known exemplars of the third redaction omit the bulk of the historical part and begin *in medias res* with the Arab invasion in the seventh millennium, focusing only on the prophetic part, much like the fourth redaction. Thus, the rearrangement of the earlier chapters does not occur in every manuscript witness of the third redaction.

109 Only the third redaction mentions explicitly the sixth millennium. The other redactions do not name the sixth millennium, although the fantastical account of Alexander the Great and his legacy in chap. 8–9 ought to fall into that period.

110 Lolos 1976 and Lolos 1978.

Table 3: Narrative speed in the *Apocalypse of Ps-Methodios.*

Chapter	Motif	Narrated time	Narrating time (word count)	Ratio
ApcMeth I				
1	first millennium	1000 years	253	0.3
2	second millennium	1000 years	168	0.2
3	third millennium	1000 years	382	0.4
4	fourth millennium	1000 years	197	0.2
5–10	fifth millennium	1000 years	2282	2.3
11–13.18	seventh millennium	unspecified	2536	N/A
13.19–21	Gog and Magog	7 years	165	23.6
13.21	savior-emperor in Jerusalem	10 ½ years	28	2.7
14.1–6	Antichrist's birth	unspecified	224	N/A
14.6–13	Antichrist's deeds	(3 ½ years)	409	(116.9)
14.14	last judgment and doxology	unspecified	67	N/A
ApcMeth II				
1	first millennium	1000 years	187	0.2
2	second millennium	1000 years	103	0.1
3	third millennium	1000 years	142	0.1
4	fourth millennium	1000 years	109	0.1
5–10	fifth millennium	1000 years	1506	1.5
11–13.18	seventh millennium	unspecified	1403	N/A
13.19–21	Gog and Magog	7 years	153	21.9
13.21	savior-emperor in Jerusalem	10 ½ years[111]	29	2.8
14.1–6	Antichrist's birth	unspecified	185	N/A
14.6–13	Antichrist's deeds	(3 ½ years)	323	(92.3)
14.14	last judgment and doxology	unspecified	60	N/A

111 Cod. Vaticanus Ottob. gr. 418, fol. 238v, saec. XV/XVI reads τῶν ι (ἥμισυ) χρόνων (10 ½ years), while codd. Ambrosianus C 92 sup., fol. 318r, saec. XIV^{MED} and Vindobonensis theol. gr. 200, fol. 130v, saec. XVI^{1} both read τοῦ ἑνὸς ἥμισυ χρόνου (1 ½ years). The latter reading seems to be a corruption of the former. The *apparatus criticus* of Lolos 1976, p. 131 is imprecise at this point.

ApcMeth III				
1	first millennium	1000 years	238	0.2
2	second millennium	1000 years	119	0.1
3	third millennium	1000 years	262	0.3
9.4, 8–9	fifth millennium	1000 years	558	0.6
4–5.5	sixth millennium	1000 years	311	0.3
5.8–13.18	seventh millennium	unspecified	2046	N/A
13.19–21	Gog and Magog	7 years	159	22.7
13.21	savior-emperor in Jerusalem	10 ½ years	64	6.1
14.1–5	Antichrist's infancy	unspecified	193	N/A
14.6–13	Antichrist's deeds	(3 ½ years)	558	(159.4)
14.14	last judgment and doxology	unspecified	42	N/A
ApcMeth IV				
10.6–13.18	seventh millennium	unspecified	2262	N/A
13.19–24	Gog and Magog	unspecified	257	N/A
13.25–28	diabolic emperor	unspecified	314	N/A

A synoptic examination of the four redactions yields the following observations concerning the velocity of the Ps-Methodian narrative. The narrative velocity of the first and second redactions is roughly identical. Both start out with a high velocity, describing millennial epochs in summary. The narrative decelerates slightly in the fifth millennium—and further still with the appearance of the Gog and Magog motif—before speeding up when portraying the Savior-Emperor's abdication. Finally, it comes to a virtual standstill when relating the deeds and destruction of the Antichrist.[112] If one wanted to illustrate these changes with a spatial analogy, one could say that the vector of time is turned into a *curve:* as the narrative approaches the *synteleia,* the increased detail causes the velocity to slow

112 The duration of the Antichrist's rule is not explicitly mentioned but was generally believed to last three and a half years, based on Dn 7:25 and Rv 11:3, 13:5. See the authoritative statements by Andrew of Caesarea (early seventh century) in Andreas Caesariensis, *In Apoc.* cap. 30 (p. 113) (comm. on Rv 11:3), cap. 36 (p. 138) (comm. on Rv 13:5), and Ps-Hippolytos (eighth century?) in Hippolytus (Ps-), *De consum.* §25, §35.

down.[113] The reader (or listener) faces an end-time scenario in which time phenomenologically decelerates with the approach of the *eschaton.*

Although the overall impression is that the narrative slows down progressively, there is a degree of fluctuation. The first three redactions of the *Apocalypse of Ps-Methodios* retain those fluctuations, which recall the irregular narrative speed in the *Apocalypse of Andrew the Fool.* Both compositions convey a pronounced irregularity in the flow of eschatological time. The remarkable thing is not that particular periods pass at different speeds. The Eastern Romans were accustomed to temporal variability. The calendrical day was divided into twelve equal parts for daytime and nighttime, which varied in length according to season.[114] An hour could last between 45 and 75 minutes in the Byzantine heartland, depending on the month. Seasonal variation and time zone differences were common knowledge in Byzantium.[115] Instead, the remarkable aspect is the rapid and continuous fluctuation in the narrative speed.

The phenomenological irregularity in temporal dilation and constriction shapes how the reader (or listener) imagines eschatological time. It produces an erratic rhythm that evoked a sense of uncertainty and curiosity about what to expect next. Such a rhythm is an aesthetic device that instills suspenseful anxiety in the audience, as volatile shifts disorient and generate a climate of precariousness that begs for clarification.[116] Arguably, the desire to overcome this disorientation reinforces any preexisting interest in prophetic lore. Thus, by creating an atmosphere of suspense, Byzantine apocalyptica further augment the reader's interest in this kind of literature.

In addition to arousing interest, the capricious changes in the narrative speed prompt the reader to engage more closely with the text. As the erratic rhythm remains unexplained, it leaves an indeterminate gap in the narrative that elicits the reader's response. The reader is forced to make sense of the strange volatility.[117]

---

113 On the arrow (or vector) of time as a hallmark of the Christian world-view, see Eco 1998, pp. 253–254 and Gurevich 1972, pp. 99–100 (translation in Gurevich 1985, pp. 110–111). Already Eusebios had compared cosmic time to a straight line (εὐθεῖαν γραμμήν), see Eusebius, *De laud. Const.* VI.4 (p. 207).

114 Rautman 2006, p. 3.

115 E.g., Symeon Seth, *Consp.* §3 (p. 19), who adduces the knowledge of different time zones to prove the spherical nature of the world.

116 Cf. Auerbach 1946, pp. 8–9, who points out that literary works create suspense by means of retarding action. The delayed action suspends the resolution of the crisis in the reader's mind, which translates into the sensation of suspense.

117 See Iser 1971, who highlights the importance of indeterminate gaps (indeterminacy) in literary works, arguing that omissions motivate the reader to participate actively in interpreting the text.

What exactly this response looked like is of secondary importance. Also, it is a risky endeavor to speculate about reader response in Byzantium, given that such effects are not only culturally conditioned but also contingent on fortuitous circumstances. Among other things, they depend on the audience's intertextual horizon of expectations, their level of tolerance for suspense, and the legibility of a particular manuscript.[118] Also, it matters whether a text is read for the first time or not, since shock effects are ephemeral and diminish when a passage is reread.[119] Although it is difficult to ascertain exactly how a Byzantine reader would have reacted to such deliberate confusion, it stands to reason that their responses varied, ranging from the sensation of helpless vulnerability to the exhilarating zeal for insurrection.[120]

2.3 Text tradition

The reader's subjective perception of eschatological time is not only influenced by the text's narrative velocity but also by the textual history. Byzantine apocalyptica are notorious for their textual fluidity and are usually passed down in different variants. As mentioned above, the open textuality is partly due to the belief in a semi-open history, which needed to be continuously rewritten and reinterpreted. In addition, the apocryphal nature encourages textual malleability. Scribes and compilers enjoyed greater liberty in emending apocrypha than canonical texts. They persistently maintained this openness and abstained from inserting prohibitions against altering the text, such as the interdiction in Rv 22:18–19, which cautions against adding anything to or removing anything from the prophecy.[121]

---

118 The legibility of a manuscript, the amount of tachygraphic abbreviations, the ductus of the scribe are medium-specific characteristics that can affect the narrative speed, as pointed out by Baetens and Hume 2006, p. 351. A similar argument can be made with regard to medium-specific characteristics when *listening* to a prophecy.

119 Iser 1971, p. 12, Hume 2005, pp. 107, 120, and Baetens and Hume 2006, p. 350.

120 Hume 2005, p. 119 argues that narrative rapidity can call forth a range of audience responses "varying from irritation and bewilderment to exhilaration". Generally, high narrative velocity is prone to incite rebellious responses in the reader, who is compelled to escape the oppression and intimidation conveyed by the fast-paced narrative (Hume 2005, p. 107). Although Hume discusses narrative speed in contemporary fiction novels, much of her analysis is applicable to Byzantine apocalyptica because the techniques of manipulating narrative speed that are at work in fiction novels can also be found in Medieval Greek apocalypses, namely (a) multiplying elements while, at the same time, (b) leaving out meaningful transitions, and (c) creating puzzling anomalies.

121 Cf. Dt 4:2, 13:1 (LXX).

The *Apocalypse of Ps-Methodios* with its four Greek redactions is just one example of the genre-specific open textuality. Many other Byzantine prophecies underwent subsequent revision. The *Prophecy of Daniel*, the *Last Vision of Daniel*, and the *Vision of Daniel on the Seven Hills* were all reworked and abridged during their transmission history. In the case of the *Prophecy of Daniel* and the *Vision of Daniel on the Seven Hills* one could even assert that they were redacted into concise oracles, which compressed the prophecies to their core idea, that of political deliverance at the hand of a messianic ruler. The following table (Table 4) gives an overview of the extent of those abridgements. Again, the word count is an estimate, which can vary from manuscript to manuscript. The titles are not included in the word count, since they exhibit great variety in the manuscript tradition.

Table 4: Word count of different redactions.

Source	Word count	Approx. date
ApcMeth I	6711	VIII^{1}
ApcMeth II	4200	XII–XIII
ApcMeth III	4550	XIV–XV
ApcMeth IV	2833	XV–XVII^{1}
ExposDan I[122]	1867	IX
ExposDan II[123]	110	XVI–XVII
UltVisDan I[124]	1035	XIII^{MED}
UltVisDan II	941	XV
VisDanSepCol I	750	XV^{2}
VisDanSepCol II	222	XVI

122 The word count is based not on D. Sakel's edition but on my collation of the three main codices: (1) Atheniensis 2187, fols 2r–5v, saec. XV^{EX}, (2) Athonensis Iberensis 181 (Lambros 4301), fols 53r–59v, saec. XVI, (3) Athonensis Xēropotamou, cod. 248 (Lambros 2581), pp. 527–532, saec. XVII.

123 This version is unpublished. The word count is based on my transcription of cod. Mancunensis gr. 22, fol. 271v, ann. 1622. The redaction is contained in at least five other manuscripts.

124 Elsewhere, I distinguished two subgroups within the first redaction of the *Last Vision of Daniel*, see Kraft 2022, pp. 347–353. However, the differences of those subgroups hardly influence the total word count.

The table shows how several historical apocalyptica were subject to later abridgement. The case of the *Apocalypse of Ps-Methodios* shows that this tendency existed already in the Byzantine period and cannot be considered solely a post-Byzantine phenomenon. Internal evidence suggests that the second Greek redaction was produced in the twelfth or thirteenth century, which is apparent from its description of battles with the "Ishmaelites" in Anatolia (*ApcMeth II*, 13.11). Those battles likely refer to historical or anticipated engagements with the Seljuqs and point to the era of the Crusades. Although the second Greek redaction adds a few new elements, it greatly condenses the whole narrative by roughly one third. The inclination for abridgement was maintained in the third redaction and continued in the fourth redaction, which reduces the text by yet another third. The fourth redaction was probably produced in the early post-Byzantine period, which is indicated by the desperate military situation vis-à-vis the Ottomans (*ApcMeth IV*, 13.11).[125]

There are various reasons for the production of abridgements of apocryphal apocalypses. First, the ambiguous and usually cryptic character of apocalyptic literature requires interpretation. One way to interpret apocalypses is to rewrite or paraphrase them. The Greek Orthodox scholar Païsios Ligaridēs (d. 1678) remarks in his renowned *Book of Prophecies* (*Χρησμολόγιον*) that "there are many obscure and enigmatic [texts], which are utterly unintelligible—they are not understood—without interpretation and paraphrase, especially [the text] of Revelation".[126] Paraphrases and abridgements require the interpretative reorganization of a text and thus lend themselves to hermeneutical study. Another factor that encourages the shortening of apocalyptic prose is the desire to recalibrate the focus of a given narrative. Over the course of time, different sections became more (or less) relevant and were thus prone to be embellished (or reduced) in size. The decline and eventual destruction of the Byzantine polity conditioned the choice to accen-

125 Later in the narrative (*ApcMeth IV*, 13.25), Ottoman hegemony is called "a satanic and wicked empire, that is, the forerunner of the Antichrist" (μία βασιλεία πονηρὰ καὶ σατανική, ἥτις ὑπάρχει πρόδρομος τοῦ ἀντιχρίστου.) – The designation "forerunner of the Antichrist" identifies the empire (βασιλεία) in question with a Muslim polity, drawing on the *locus classicus* by Ioannis Damascinus, *De haer.* cap. 100 (p. 60, ll. 1–2), who identified the "deceitful worship of the Ishmaelites" (λαοπλανὴς θρησκεία τῶν Ἰσμαηλιτῶν, i.e., Islam) with the "forerunner of the Antichrist". The earliest dated text witness of the fourth redaction is cod. Mancunensis gr. 22, fols 259r–266v, ann. 1622. Thus, the final redaction was composed sometime between the fifteenth and early seventeenth century.

126 Cod. Hierosolymitanus S. Sepulcri gr. 160, fol. 224v, ann. 1656: πολλὰ εἶναι δυσνόητα καὶ γριφώδη, τὰ ὁποῖα χωρὶς ἑρμηνείαν καὶ παράφρασιν δὲν νοοῦνται ποσῶς, δὲν καταλαμβάνονται, καὶ μάλιστα τῆς ἀποκαλύψεως. – The passage has been transcribed and translated by Pissis 2021, p. 307. I have introduced minor changes.

tuate political redemption as the core message of Byzantine prophecies.[127] Third, the economic factor may also have played a role in the production of abridged prophecies. The financial incentive to minimize production costs in terms of scribal labor and writing material must have been a concern that many copyists and scholars had to take into consideration. A short prophecy was cheaper and quicker to produce than a full-length apocalypse.

The demand for and availability of prophetic literature changed over time. In general, it can be asserted that apocalyptic literature was particularly popular during periods of perceived hardship and crisis. The Ottoman conquest of Constantinople (1453) certainly marked such a period. We have the notable testimony by a certain Dēmētrios (PLP 5256), who wrote a letter to his brother in Christ Manouēl in July 1453, asking for a copy of the *Apocalypse of Ps-Methodios*, for "either the old or a more recent one".[128] Dēmētrios' letter testifies not only to the interest in the *Apocalypse of Ps-Methodios* in the mid-fifteenth century but also to the awareness that different variants of the text were in circulation.

The heightened interest in apocalyptic literature is also evident by the sharp increase in manuscript copies as well as in the production of specialized compilations.[129] A large number of apocalyptic anthologies (χρησμολόγια) was produced in the early post-Byzantine period. Those anthologies collected, arranged, and up-

127 The long reception history of the *Apocalypse of Ps-Methodios* shows that it was not always read as a political prophecy. Palmer 2014, pp. 126–129 has argued that it was initially—in the eighth century and in the Latin West —read as a *moralizing* (and not politicizing) prophecy. An unedited collection of diverse scholia in an eleventh-century manuscript from Byzantine Italy (cod. Vaticanus Reg. gr. Pio II 22, fol. 69v) contains an excerpt from the *Apocalypse of Ps-Methodios* (*ApcMeth I*, 14.6–8). The excerpt quotes Ps-Methodios' exegesis of Gn 49:17, arguing that this biblical verse proves that the Antichrist would descend from the tribe of Dan. Here, the *exegetical* utility of the text was highlighted.

128 Demetrius, *Epist.* p. 91, ll. 8–10: Παρακαλῶ τὴν ἀντίληψίν σου πάμπολλα ἵνα μοι ἀποστείλῃς τὸ βιβλίον τοῦ ἁγίου Μεθοδίου τοῦ Πατάρων, ἢ τὸ ἄρχαιον ἢ καὶ νεόγραφον, ἐὰν ἔχῃς· | I greatly ask for your understanding to send me the book of Saint Methodios of Patara, either the old or a more recent one, if you have it. – The book in question is, in all likelihood, the *Apocalypse of Ps-Methodios*, given the historical context of the recent Fall of Constantinople to the Ottomans (May 29, 1453) and the fact that no other work by Methodios would have enjoyed the prestige to serve as a soothing gesture in a hostage situation.

129 Little is known about the manuscript transmission of Byzantine apocalyptica during the Byzantine period. The large majority of the manuscripts that have survived were copied in the post-Byzantine period, especially between the fifteenth and seventeenth centuries. Taking the *Apocalypse of Ps-Methodios* as an example, only three of the forty known manuscripts predate the fifteenth century. These are: codd. (1) Ambrosianus C 92 sup. (Martini/Bassi 192), fols 313r–318v, saec. XIV^{MED}, (2) Athonensis Iberensis 349 (Lambros 4469), fols 1r–20v, saec. XIV, and (3) Vaticanus gr. 1700, fols 117r–157r, ann. 1332/33.

dated Byzantine texts, presenting a series of successive prophecies that focus on the emergence of a messianic ruler and the recovery of Constantinople.[130] Those texts frequently omit the Antichrist figure and the Last Judgment. When reading such an anthology—and not just any particular text—one finds a mantra-like repetition of imperial ideology. The imminent resurrection of the Orthodox polity received unrivaled attention, with the result that explicit references to the *eschaton* were mitigated.[131]

Arguably, the concatenation of apocalyptic narratives demands a different reader engagement, given that a series of related prophecies generally requires less interpretative effort than isolated or dispersed texts.[132] Thus, by repeatedly privileging the theme of immediate worldly restoration, the anthologies diminished the need for active reader participation and, more importantly, marginalized the Last Judgment motif. In this way, political redemption eclipsed the prospect of eschatological salvation.

The abridgements of Byzantine apocalyptica signified a subtle shift in temporal perception. Lettered contemporaries, such as the aforementioned Dēmētrios, would have noted that abridged political prophecies compress the narrative and thereby accelerate time. Others, who read or listened to the later abridgements only, would have noticed a pronounced emphasis on immediate change. A brief and uplifting forecast renders the resolution of crisis significantly closer than does an elaborate and panoramic world history. A decrease in length also curtails the effectiveness of literary techniques. While a long prophecy can readily employ literary methods to accelerate or decelerate the narrative, a short redaction has limited scope for such techniques. The reduction in size also went hand in hand with an increasing inattentiveness to other motifs of the apocalyptic script. The gradual shift from grand narratives to situational pronouncements limited the author's literary maneuverability and conveyed a time perception that was detached from the *synteleia*. In other words, historical apocalyptica were rewritten to omit much of the narrative paraphernalia that had buttressed global apocalyptic visions and to focus instead on the imminent resurrection of the Greek Orthodox polity.[133] To use a modern analogy, the hyper-accelerated narratives of late

---

130 See Hatzopoulos 2009, Guran 2014, and Pissis 2014, who discuss the gradual accentuation of political redemption in late and post-Byzantine apocalyptica.

131 Pertinent examples are codd. Athonensis Iberensis 686 (Lambros 4806), fols 5r–23r, saec. XVII, Hauniensis GKS 2147 4°, fols 1r–23r, saec. XVI², Mancunensis gr. 22, fols 259r–286r, ann. 1622, Marcianus gr. IV.46 (coll. 1464), pp. 322–346, saec. XVII, and Vindobonensis suppl. gr. 172, fols 1r–77v, saec. XVI.

132 Cf. Iser 1971, p. 17.

133 Examples of this development are *ApcMeth IV*, *IntrpGenSch*, and *UltVisDan II*.

Byzantine apocalyptica are more akin to snapshots of instantaneous redemption than to continuous films of providential history. Implicit in this development is a gradual shift in apocalyptic time away from the progressively unfolding mytho-historical timeline of human salvation towards episodic and myopic tales of collective revival. The *eschaton* became gradually subordinated to the typological resuscitation of the New Israel; it was deferred to the time after the political liberation from the perceived new captivity and exile.

3 Typology

Ceci nous montre la relation organique
qui unit typologie et prophétie, τύπος et λόγος.
Ce ne sont pu en réalité choses distinctes, mais
la prophétie est déjà interprétation typologique de l'histoire.[134]
Jean Daniélou

The sequence of the apocalyptic script is structured according to two persistent patterns: I) the vector of time, which is directed at the *eschaton*, and II) biblical typology, which transcends the linear thread of time and bestows providential significance to particular events. Biblical typology is a hermeneutical method that assigns correspondences among discrete characters and occurrences. A given correspondence amounts to a set of counterparts that are dispersed throughout time and that refer to one another in a reciprocal manner. This reciprocity is qualified insofar as earlier actors or events (*types*) adumbrate their subsequent counterparts (*antitypes*), which, in turn, complete their premonitory heralds.[135] Typology establishes a unidirectional trajectory towards the future and assigns axiological value to the vector of time: the further an event or character is placed along the vector, the higher its moral import and providential significance. That is why, Byzantine apocalyptica persistently stress that the ferocity and gravity of eschatological events will be unprecedented.[136] In essence, typology is a medium of completion and denotes progressive escalation with world-historical significance.[137] This chapter shows that Byzantine apocalyptica adopted standard scriptural typologies as well as devised new ones. In particular, it explores the typologies of the Savior-Emperor and the Antichrist. Moreover, it applies the Bakhtinian notion of chronotope to explain how typology functions as a chronotopic device that fundamentally shapes the structure of apocalyptic time.

134 Daniélou 1950, p. 135.

135 On *types* and *antitypes* in biblical hermeneutics, see Auerbach 1938, pp. 450–464 (translation in Auerbach 1984, pp. 28–49), Vos 1948, pp. 161–164, and Kannengiesser 2004, pp. 228–232.

136 *ApcAndr* ll. 3861–62: οἷα οὐ γέγονεν ἀπ' ἀρχῆς κόσμου οὐδ' οὐ μὴ γενήσεται | such as has not happened since the beginning of the world and will never happen again – *DiegDan* §§6.1, 11.29, 11.37, 12.9: οἷα οὐ γέγονεν ἀπὸ καταβολῆς κόσμου | such as has not happened since the foundation of the world. – Cf. Dn 12:1, Jl 2:2, Mt 24:21, Mk 13:19, Rv 13:8.

137 See Daniélou 1950, p. 72, Goppelt 1964, p. 330, Davidson 1981, p. 398, Guinot 1989, pp. 21–22, and Ninow 2001, pp. 153–156, *passim*.

https://doi.org/10.1515/9783112230114-005

3.1 Scriptural figures

Typology forms an essential part of biblical hermeneutics. It was already used in the Old Testament.[138] The New Testament continued the technique and constructed new typological correspondences that sought to prove the fulfillment of the Old Covenant in Christ. The focal point of virtually every biblical typology is Christ,[139] in whom the final consummation was expected to take place.[140] This Christocentric orientation was succinctly expressed by Nicholas Kabasilas (d. c. 1392), who at the outset of his *Second Oration on Ezekiel* points out that: "Every prophecy, contemplation, and vision were images of the coming of the Savior; and the whole Old Testament ultimately refers to it."[141] Accordingly, Christ has been presented as a New Adam (Rom 5:14), a New David (Mt 1:1–17, Acts 2:29–32), a New Jonah (Mt 12:39–41, Lk 11:29–32), and the like. In early Christianity, this coherence was challenged by Gnostic and Jewish dissensions, which prompted further typological exegesis.[142] But typology served not only apologetic means in the patristic period. It was also employed in catechesis, sermons, iconography as well as in scriptural commentaries, hagiography, and historiography.[143] By such means of habitual application, typology evolved into "a mode of thought and [...] figure of speech",[144] which was pervasive and ubiquitous.

Typological hermeneutics originated in biblical exegesis and gradually expanded into other literary genres. New, extra-biblical types were introduced, such as Alexander the Great and Constantine the Great. It is critical to note that typological reasoning did not end with the last book of the Bible, nor did it

---

138 See Goppelt 1966, pp. 23–47, Davidson 2011, pp. 12 36, and Ninow 2001.

139 Davidson 1981, pp. 399–400. Similarly, Krueger 2004, p. 17.

140 See 1 Cor 10:11: ταῦτα δὲ *τυπικῶς* συνέβαινεν ἐκείνοις, ἐγράφη δὲ πρὸς νουθεσίαν ἡμῶν, εἰς οὓς τὰ τέλη τῶν αἰώνων κατήντηκεν. | All these things happened unto them as *foreshadowings*, and they were written for our admonition, on whom the ends of the ages have come. (italics and translation mine) – For commentary, see Davidson 1981, pp. 193–297.

141 Nicolaus Cabasilas, *Orat.* 2, p. 71: Πᾶσα προφητεία καὶ θεωρία καὶ ὅρασις εἰκόνες ἦσαν τῆς τοῦ σωτῆρος ἐπιδημίας· καὶ πᾶσα δὲ Γραφὴ παλαιὰ πρὸς αὐτήν, καθάπερ εἰς τέλος, τὴν ἀναφορὰν ἔχει. – For commentary, see Congourdeau 2018.

142 See Daniélou 1950, pp. x–xi and Guinot 1989, p. 33.

143 Daniélou 1950, pp. xi–xvi. On the use of typologies in the hymnography of Romanos the Melodist and Leontios the Presbyter, see Krueger 2014, pp. 67–105 and Gador-Whyte 2017, pp. 54–101. For its use in hagiography, see Delouis 2003, pp. 246–247. On typology in historiography, see Torgerson 2022, pp. 136–141.

144 Frye 1982, p. 80. Similarly, Goppelt 1964, p. 332 referred to typology as a "pneumatische Betrachtungsweise", Krueger 2004, p. 27 called it a "biblicizing worldview", and Holdenried 2017, p. 28 labeled it a "habit of mind".

cease after the patristic period.[145] It remained a living tradition throughout the Byzantine millennium and beyond, especially in prophetic writings. Byzantine apocalyptists continuously incorporated traditional typologies and devised new ones when (re)constructing the history of the future.

Byzantine apocalyptica regularly integrated New Testament typologies that expected key Old Testament events to find their fulfillment at the *eschaton*. One such typology is based on Mt 24:37–38 and Lk 17:26–27, where Christ's Second Coming is likened to the unsuspecting peace and quiet that preceded the Great Flood (Gn 6–9). Byzantine political prophecies recurrently used this typology, envisioning the fulfillment of the antediluvian calm in an eschatological tranquility. The motif appears in the *Apocalypse of Ps-Methodios* and the apocalyptic section in the *Life of Andrew the Fool*.[146] Both texts associate the blissful period with the reign of a messianic emperor, diverging from the original Gospel typology, which centers exclusively on Christ.[147] Ps-Methodios and Andrew the Fool thus altered the typology, supplanting Christ with an ideal Roman emperor who functions as Christ's surrogate. Moreover, they leave aside the original context of the passage, which pertains to the unknown hour of Christ's return, and instead focus on the original joy and peace of the primordial era. This recalibration allowed for the seamless integration of the scriptural typology into the timeline of the Byzantine apocalyptic script.

The Great Flood typology was also picked up by the anonymous author of the *Prediction of Andritzopoulos*. This thirteenth-century apocalyptic prognostication likens the anticipated *eschaton* to Noah's times by asserting that the dissolution of both the Roman Empire and the Church would not occur abruptly but piecemeal, "just as in the time of Noah, [when] the Flood happened little by little and not suddenly".[148] According to the Genesis story (Gn 7:12, 17), it took forty days and nights of torrential rain for the earth to be flooded and Noah's ark to be set afloat. The *Prediction of Andritzopoulos* likens the gradual submergence of the earth to the gradual but ultimate collapse of the Christian Roman Empire. It is noteworthy that the prophecy identifies both the Orthodox Church *and* the

---

145 For patristic typology, see Daniélou 1950. For a useful bibliographical overview, see further Kannengiesser 2004, pp. 238–242.

146 *ApcMeth I*, 13.17 (ὥσπερ γὰρ ἐν ταῖς ἡμέραις τοῦ Νῶε) – *ApcMeth II*, 13.17 (ὥσπερ ἐν ταῖς ἡμέραις) – *ApcMeth III*, 13.17 (ὥσπερ γὰρ ἦσαν ἐν ταῖς ἡμέραις πρὸ τοῦ κατακλυσμοῦ) – *ApcAndr* ll. 3826–27 (ὡς ἐπὶ τοῦ Νῶε τὰ ἔτη), ll. 3857–58 (ἐπὶ τοῦ Νῶε ἐν ἠρεμίᾳ).

147 As already noted by Alexander 1985, pp. 160, 169 and Rydén 1995, II, p. 346, n. 10.

148 *PraedAndritz* l. 16: [...] ὥσπερ γέγονε καὶ ὁ κατακλυσμὸς ἐπὶ τοῦ Νῶε κατ’ ὀλίγον καὶ οὐκ ἐξάπινα [...].

Roman Empire with the force that withholds the Antichrist.[149] This identification is both traditional and innovative. On the one hand, it follows the traditional Byzantine ideology that identified Roman rule with the fourth Danielic animal and, hence, with the last kingdom on earth.[150] On the other, the pairing of the Church *and* Empire as two factors that constitute Roman rule gives an unusual equal footing to both institutions. This new interpretation of the "withholding force" (κατέχον) may have been inspired by historical realities as well as by the dual nature of the biblical motif of the fourth Danielic kingdom, which is said to consist of two parts, iron and clay (Dn 2:33–34, 41–42). In any event, the *Prediction of Andritzopoulos* presents the gradually appearing Great Flood in the Old Testament as an adumbration for the progressively subsiding Christian Roman rule at the *eschaton.*

The biblically literate Byzantines knew that God promised not to destroy the world ever again by means of a great deluge (Gn 9:11, 15). Yet the world had to be destroyed eventually. This raised the question of how, if not by the waters of a flood. One answer was to envision the eschatological cataclysm as the typological escalation of the destruction wrought by the plagues of Egypt (Ex 7–11). The *Book of Revelation* contains an Exodus typology that predicted how some of the ten plagues of Egypt would be repeated and intensified prior to the Second Coming.[151] One of those typologically constructed afflictions was the locust plague (Rv 9:3).

The notion of an eschatological locust plague appears prominently in the *Apocalypse of Ps-Methodios* and the *Last Vision of Daniel.* The former text uses the image of locusts to describe the Midianites, who are cast as the typological predecessors of the seventh-century Arabs.[152] On the basis of Gn 37:28 and Jgs 8:24, Ps-Methodios equates the Midianites, who are said to have conquered the known world in Old Testament times, with the Arabs, who took control of vast territories of the Byzantium Empire in the seventh century AD. Later in the narra-

149 *PraedAndritz* ll. 10–12: κατέχον δὲ λέγει τὴν τῶν Ῥωμαίων ἀρχήν· [...] σωζομένης γὰρ τῆς ἐκκλησίας καὶ τῆς βασιλείας τῶν εὐσεβῶν, ὁ διάβολος οὐκ ἐλεύσεται, [...] | He [i. e., Paul] declares the withholding force [2 Thes 2:6–7] the rule of the Romans. [...] For as long as the church and the kingdom of the pious [Christians] are preserved, the devil will not come [...] – A. Rigo's edition contains a typo: instead of τοῦ Ῥωμαίων, the text should read τῶν Ῥωμαίων, which is also the reading that the manuscript provides (cod. Parisinus gr. 2661, fol. 208v, ann. 1364).

150 See above note 66. For a general overview of the reception history of the Four-Kingdoms motif, see Breed 2014. For specific case studies, see Perrin and Stuckenbruck 2021.

151 Hail (Rv 8:7, cf. Ex 9:22), turning the sea into blood (Rv 8:8, 16:3–4, cf. Ex 7:20), darkness (Rv 8:12, 16:10, cf. Ex 10:21), and locusts (Rv 9:3, cf. Ex 10:12). See Goppelt 1966, p. 238, Daniélou 1950, p. 142, and Boxall 2023, p. 570. On the use of the Exodus typology in earlier biblical prophecies, see Daniélou 1950, pp. 131–135 and Ninow 2001, pp. 157–241.

152 *ApcMeth I–II*, 5.3. See Reinink 1982, pp. 339–342 and Suermann 1987, p. 334.

tive, Ps-Methodios repeats the typology to make utterly clear that the Arabs are the new locust plague.[153] The typology thus runs as follows in the *Apocalypse of Ps-Methodios:* the locust scourge started with the eighth plague of Egypt (Ex 10:1–20), reached a preliminary *crescendo* in the conquests of the Midianites (Jgs 6:1–6, *ApcMeth I*, 5.3), and found its penultimate climax in the Arab occupation of the Near East (*ApcMeth I*, 11.13). The locust typology reappears towards the end of the *Apocalypse of Ps-Methodios*, where it is used to express the notion of a plentiful repopulation of the deserted world.[154] That is to say, Ps-Methodios' last usage of the typology inverts the disparaging image of locusts and gives it a tentatively positive meaning.[155] The ultimate antitype of the locust typology is an eschatological abundance, which functions as the prelude to the aforementioned typology of the antediluvian calm. Ps-Methodios thus juxtaposes two scriptural typologies and reveals their almost synchronous culmination at the *eschaton* (*ApcMeth I–II*, 13.15, 13.17).

The locust typology also appears in the *Last Vision of Daniel*, which was written in response to the sack and occupation of Constantinople in 1204 at the hands of the Fourth Crusade.[156] The Fourth Crusade gave new immediacy to Old Testament typologies, as many Eastern Romans found themselves either subjugated by a foreign power or forced into exile. The desire to remove the yoke of foreign oppression and to return to Constantinople, the New Jerusalem, stands behind the many Exodus and Exile typologies of the thirteenth century.[157] The *Last Vision of Daniel* is a typical product of the period. Its opening lines paraphrase Rv 8–9, interpreting the calamities brought about by the first four apocalyptic angels (Rv 8:7–12) with a reference to afflictions that different regions of the Byzantine Empire had suffered.[158] It then adopts the typology of Rv 9:1–11, in which a fifth

---

153 *ApcMeth I*, 11.13 and *ApcMeth IV*, 11.13 quoting Jgs 6:5, 7:12.

154 *ApcMeth I–II*, 13.15, and *ApcMeth IV*, 13.15.

155 For completeness it should be noted that the locust motif appears again in *ApcMeth IV*, 13.24, where it is applied to the Gog and Magog text-block, reverting to the pejorative meaning.

156 I agree with Wortley 1977, pp. 8–9 and Brandes 2007, p. 253, who date the text to the thirteenth century. For an overview of other dating attempts, see Kraft 2018a, p. 115.

157 See Magdalino and Nelson 2010, pp. 25–26. Moses (Exodus) and Zorobabel (Exile) typologies were frequently conflated, e.g., in Nikētas Chōniatēs' *History* and panegyrics, see Nicetas Choniates, *Hist.* p. 356, l. 33, p. 578, l. 45 and Nicetas Choniates, *Orat.* p. 147, ll. 1–7 (*Orat.* 14), p. 160, ll. 19–20 (*Orat.* 15). See further Angelov 2007, pp. 86, 98–99. Among Byzantine apocalyptica, the Moses typology appears explicitly in the thirteenth-century *NarrMend* ll. 19–20. On the Jerusalemization of Constantinople, see Congourdeau 2001, Meyer 2009, Erdeljan 2017, pp. 72–143, and Magdalino 2021, pp. 24–25.

158 *UltVisDan I*, §§3–10.

angel brings about a new locust scourge.[159] The biblical typology modifies a central aspect of the original Egyptian scourge (Ex 10:5), insofar as the locusts are said *not* to destroy any vegetation but only the people not elected by God (Rv 9:4), which the *Last Vision of Daniel* identifies with unrepentant sinners.[160] By adopting the locust typology and by placing it prior to the description of the fall of Constantinople in the historical part of the prophecy, the pseudonymous author declares this biblical prophecy to be fulfilled and implicitly identifies the soldiers of the Fourth Crusade with a swarm of locusts.[161] In sum, Byzantine apocalyptica regularly drew on biblical typologies, such as a new antediluvian calm and a new locust plague, and weaved them into the apocalyptic script of the New Rome.[162]

3.2 Christological types

Medieval Greek apocalyptica not only adopted typologies from the Scriptures but also devised new ones. Byzantine apocalypses faithfully continued the Christocentrism of typological hermeneutics and constructed new literary figures in explicit

---

159 *UltVisDan I*, §§11–13: καὶ οὐαί σοι γῆ ἐκ τῶν βασάνων ὧν μέλλει ἐξαποστεῖλαι κύριος παντοκράτωρ ἐπί σε. *ἀκρίδας* ἀγρίας καὶ ἀναιμάκτους μέλλει πέμψαι ἐπί σε. *καὶ οὔτε ζῶον οὔτε δένδρον μέλλουσιν ἅψασθαι* εἰ μὴ τοὺς μὴ μετανοήσαντας διὰ τὰς πολλὰς αὐτῶν ἀνομίας καὶ ἀδικίας. | And woe to you, earth, because of the trials that the Lord Almighty will send forth against you. He will send against you wild and bloodless *locusts. And they will not touch either animal or tree* but only those who did not repent for their great lawlessness and injustice. – Unfortunately, the oldest textual witness, cod. Vaticanus gr. 1700, fol. 100v, ann. 1332/33, is corrupt at the beginning, and the key term ἀκρίδας is not legible. Alternative readings include cod. Oxoniensis Baroc. gr. 145, fol. 61v and 96v, saec. XVI. ἀκρίδας τρίας ἀναιμάκτους ("three bloodless locusts") or cod. Guelferbytanus Gud. gr. 9, fol. 16v, saec. XVII: ἀκρίδας ἀγρίας καὶ ἀναιδεστάτους ("wild and most shameless locusts"). These variations do not, however, affect the typology under discussion. For further discussion of this passage, see Silvano 2025, p. 236.

160 *UltVisDan I*, §13: καὶ οὔτε ζῶον οὔτε δένδρον μέλλουσιν ἅψασθαι εἰ μὴ τοὺς μὴ μετανοήσαντας διὰ τὰς πολλὰς αὐτῶν ἀνομίας καὶ ἀδικίας. | And they will not touch either animal or tree but only those who did not repent for their great lawlessness and injustice. – Rv 9:4 καὶ ἐρρέθη αὐταῖς ἵνα μὴ ἀδικήσουσι τὸν χόρτον τῆς γῆς οὐδὲ πᾶν χλωρὸν οὐδὲ πᾶν δένδρον, εἰ μὴ τοὺς ἀνθρώπους οἵτινες οὐκ ἔχουσι τὴν σφραγῖδα τοῦ θεοῦ ἐπὶ τῶν μετώπων. | And it was commanded them that they should not hurt the grass of the earth, neither any green thing, neither any tree; but only those men which have not the seal of God in their foreheads. – Ex 10:5 […] καὶ κατέδεται πᾶν ξύλον τὸ φυόμενον ὑμῖν ἐπὶ τῆς γῆς· | […] and [the locusts] shall eat every tree which groweth for you out of the field.

161 It should be remembered that already Anna Komnēnē—in the mid-twelfth century—associated the armies of the First Crusade with locusts, see Anna Comnena, *Alex.* 10.5.7–8 (p. 298). For the date of the *Alexiad*, see Magdalino 2000b and Stephenson 2003.

162 For further examples, see Kraft 2017, pp. 77–78 and Kraft 2018c, p. 187.

reference to Christ. The most pervasive Christomimetic typologies are the Savior-Emperor and the Antichrist, both individual actors that are modeled on Christ's salvific actions. The Savior-Emperor is shown to emulate Christ's meekness, self-sacrifice, and resurrection, while the *Anti*-Christ is shown to invert Christ's genuine miracles and teachings. The two literary figures form two sides of the same coin. The Savior-Emperor constitutes Christ's thetical antitype, whereas the Antichrist is His antithetical antitype. Put differently, typological correspondences are either positive or antithetical.[163] The possibility of altering the semantics of a particular antitype and inverting the axiological verdict associated with it generates much of the vitality and ambivalence of apocalyptic literature. The following examples illustrate this dynamism.

The *topos* of the Savior-Emperor appears in most political prophecies from Byzantium. It consists of a variable range of semantic layers that renders the *topos* a composite text-block rather than a singular motif.[164] It draws on an array of allusions to mytho-historical characters, first and foremost, to Alexander and Constantine the Great. The Savior-Emperor is typologically cast into the role of New Alexander and New Constantine, whose task is to reconstitute the imperial legacy and imagined apogee of the Greco-Roman past.[165] More importantly, the text-block aligns with biblical accounts of Christ's deeds, death, and resurrection. Those accounts are adapted to an anticipated political savior who typologically augments Christ's achievements—most notably His resurrection—in preparation for the Second Coming. As such, the Savior-Emperor *topos* is not only a key typological construct but also a classic case of Christomimesis.[166]

---

163 Goppelt 1964, p. 331.

164 Cf. the diagram by Greisiger 2014, p. 179, which illustrates different layers of the *topos*.

165 For the typology of a New Alexander, see *ApcMeth I–III*, 8–9, 13.19–21, *ApcMeth IV*, 13.19–24. See further Alexander 1985, pp. 18–19, 185–189, *passim* and Reinink 2002. Generally, on Alexander the Great in Byzantium and the Syriac world, see Kaldellis 2022 and Debié 2024. For examples when the Savior-Emperor is presented as a New Constantine, see *UltVisDan I*, §§50–51: καὶ δώσουσιν εἰς τὴν δεξιὰν αὐτοῦ χεῖρα ῥομφαίαν λέγοντες αὐτῷ· ἀνδρίζου καὶ νίκα τοὺς ἐχθρούς σου. | And they [i.e., angels] will give a sword into his right hand and say to him: take courage and vanquish your enemies! – *VisDanSepCol I*, §2.8: καὶ τὴν ῥάβδον τοῦ θεοῦ καὶ μάχαιραν δώσουσιν αὐτῷ καὶ εἴπωσι· λαβὲ καὶ ἐν τούτῳ νίκα τοὺς ἐχθρούς σου. | And they [i.e., angels] will give the scepter of God and a dagger to him and say: take [them] and by this vanquish your enemies! – Cf. Eusebius, *Vit. Const.* 1.28.2 (p. 30).

166 The literature on Christomimesis is substantial. With regard to Byzantine political ideology, see Ostrogorsky 1956, pp. 2–5, Runciman 1977, pp. 1–2, 22, 46, Marsengill 2013, pp. 283–293, Ahrweiler 1996, and Magdalino 2017, pp. 580–585. On Christomimesis in Byzantine art and on seals, see Maguire 1997 and Cotsonis 2013. For a thought-provoking distinction between the 'mimesis' and the 'following' of Christ, see Ong 1994, who observes that Christ does not ask to be imitated in the Gospels, but to be followed. Consequently, the term Christomimesis may be-

The Christ-like nature of the Savior-Emperor is constructed primarily in reference to the Holy Writ. Prominent elements are the miraculous appearance, self-sacrifice, and triumph over God's enemies. The Savior-Emperor is described to 'rise suddenly' and in an unexpected manner, like the risen Christ.[167] The verb habitually used to express the appearance of the Savior-Emperor is either ἀνίστημι (to rise) or ἐγείρω (to raise up), which echoes the Gospel accounts of the resurrection.[168] To amplify the allusion, the Savior-Emperor is said to appear "like from the dead".[169] This locution became a shorthand expression for the messianic emperor in Byzantine and post-Byzantine apocalypses. Another frequently

—technically speaking—misleading, as it can suggest mechanical reproduction (mimesis) rather than the organic supplement to (or typological fulfillment of) Christ's life and deeds. Corroborative evidence can be found in the fact that the verb "to imitate" (μιμέομαι) is rarely used in Byzantine apocalyptica, and when it does appear, it is only in a pejorative sense, see below note 214. In response to Ong's observation, I use the term 'Christomimesis' to denote the selective and adaptive (rather than purely mechanical) appropriation of Christ-like characteristics.

167 *ApcMeth* I, 13.11: τότε *αἰφνίδιον* ἐπελεύσονται ἐπ' αὐτοὺς θλῖψις καὶ στενοχωρία, καὶ ἐξελεύσεται ἐπ' αὐτοὺς βασιλεὺς Ἑλλήνων, ἤτοι Ῥωμαίων, [...] | Then *suddenly* affliction and distress will come upon them [i. e., the Ishmaelites], and the king of the Greeks, that is of the Romans, will march out against them [...] – The oldest manuscript witness (cod. Vaticanus gr. 1700, fol. 148v, ann. 1323/33) reads ἐπαναστήσεται instead of ἐξελεύσεται (the former was chosen by Lolos 1976, p. 122, l. 55). The expression ἐπαναστήσεται (he will rise up) further amplifies the prophetic tone, echoing Is 31:2. See further *AnonymVatic* p. 48, ll. 27–28: καὶ *ἐξαναστήσεται αἰφνιδίως* (cod. εὐνίδιος) βασιλεὺς δίκαιος ἀφωμοιωμένος τῷ υἱῷ τοῦ θεοῦ [...] | and *suddenly* a righteous king *will rise up*, made like unto the Son of God [...] – *ApcAndr* ll. 3824–25: *Ἀναστήσει* κύριος ὁ θεὸς ἐν ταῖς ἐσχάταις ἡμέραις βασιλείαν ἀπὸ πενίας [...] | The Lord God *will raise up* an emperor from poverty in the last days [...] – *DiegDan* §5.5: καὶ *ἐγείρει* κύριος βασιλέα τῶν Ῥωμαίων [...] | And the Lord *will raise up* a king of the Romans [...].

168 For ἀνίστημι, see Mk 16:9, Lk 24:46, Jn 20:9. For ἐγείρω, see Mt 28:7, Mk 16:6, Lk 24:34. To be sure, these verbs were also used to describe other eschatological emperors, who are to appear either prior to or after the Savior-Emperor. However, when viewed together with other messianic characteristics, these verbs acquire a soteriological meaning.

169 *ApcMeth* I, 13.11: [...] ὃν ἐλογίζοντο οἱ ἄνθρωποι ὡσεὶ *νεκρὸν ὄντα* καὶ εἰς οὐδὲν χρησιμεύοντα· | [...] whom people have considered *to be dead* and good for nothing. – *VisDanSepCol I*, §2.6: καὶ αὐτὸς [ὡς] *ἐκ τῶν νεκρῶν* ἐμφανισθήσεται | and he will appear *like from the dead*. – *DiegDan* §5.5: ὅνπερ λέγουσιν οἱ ἄνθρωποι *νεκρὸν* ὄντα καὶ εἰς οὐδὲν χρησιμεύοντα, ὅνπερ νομίζουσιν οἱ ἄνθρωποι πρὸ πολλῶν χρόνων ἀποθανόντα. | whom they say is *dead* and useful for nothing, whom people think died many years ago. – *Ps-Chrys* §5.2: ὃν εἶχον οἱ ἄνθρωποι ὡσεὶ *νεκρὸν* καὶ οὐδὲν χρησιμεύοντα. | whom people considered *dead* and good for nothing – *VisioDan* §2.5: [...] ὃν ἐδόκουν οἱ ἄνθρωποι ὡς *νεκρὸν* εἶναι καὶ οὐδὲν χρησιμεύειν. | [...] whom people thought to be *dead* and good for nothing. – *NarrMend* l. 53: τὸν *νεκρὸν* ὄντα τῷ σώματι, κ(αὶ) ἔνπνουν καὶ ζῶντα τῷ πν(εύματ)ι· | [he] is *dead* in body but breathing and alive in spirit – *NarrMend* ll. 39–40 and ll. 102–103. See further *OracLeon* p. 64, l. 9 (Orac. 4), p. 80, l. 4 (Orac. 12), p. 82, l. 2 (Orac. 13), p. 84, l. 9 (Orac. 14).

used element was the humble origin of the Savior-Emperor, which recalls Christ's nativity (Lk 2:6–7) and his promotion of poverty and meekness in the Sermon on the Mount (Mt 5:3–12, cf. Lk 6:20–23).[170] Alternatively, some prophecies emphasize his "hidden" nature, specifying that the Savior-Emperor's name and provenance was previously concealed and hence unknown.[171] Allusions to hiddenness and concealment fit well the apocalyptic genre, which professes to reveal arcane secrets. Moreover, the notion of hiddenness may be inspired by the scriptural expectation that the Messiah's origin would be unknown (Jh 7:27) as well as by Christ's unforeseen epiphany at His baptism (Mt 3:13–17, Mk 1:9–11, Lk 3:21–22). The expectation that the political savior would emulate Christ's initially "hidden" nature is voiced particularly in late Byzantine apocalypses, which portray the appearance of the messianic emperor as a veritable epiphany.[172] Other elements were on occasion added to buttress the providential nature of the Savior-Emperor's arrival, such as earthquakes, which recall Christ's resurrection based on Mt 28:2.[173]

In conjunction with his miraculous appearance stands the Savior-Emperor's voluntary abdication, which is presented as the typological antitype of Christ's self-sacrifice on the cross. The notion of an imperial abdication seems to have

---

170 *Ps-Chrys* §5.1: [...] οὔτινος τὸ ὄνομα ἦν *ἔλαττον* ἐν τῷ κόσμῳ. | [...] whose name was *inferior* in the world. – *ApcAndr* ll. 3824–25: Ἀναστήσει κύριος ὁ θεὸς ἐν ταῖς ἐσχάταις ἡμέραις βασιλείαν *ἀπὸ πενίας* [...] | The Lord God will raise up an emperor *from poverty* in the last days [...] – *NarrMend* l. 1: Περὶ τοῦ θρηλλουμένου *πτωχοῦ* καὶ ἐκλεκτοῦ βασιλέως· | About the famed, *poor*, and chosen emperor. – *AenigLeon* p. 101, ll. 335 (Or. 1): ὁ πτχωὸς ὁ Πτωχολέων | The poor, the Poor-Lion – *VisDanSanHom* ll. 400–402: Τῷ δὲ ἁγίῳ ἱερομάρτυρι Μεθοδίῳ Πατάρων οὕτως εἴρηται· ὅτι μετὰ τὸν ἔκδημον βοῦν, ἤτοι τὸν *ἐκ πενίας* ἀναστησόμενον βασιλέα [...] | The holy Hieromartyr Methodios of Patara thus said that after the departed bull, that is, the king who will rise *from poverty* [...] – *VisDanSepCol I*, §2.5: καὶ ὁ λέων *πτωχὸς* ἐμφανισθήσεται [...] | and the *poor* lion will appear [...].

171 *SibTibGr* l. 163: τὸ δὲ ὄνομα τοῦ βασιλέως *κεκρυμμένον* ἐστὶ τοῖς ἔθνεσιν [...] | The name of the king is *hidden* from the nations [...] – *NarrMend* ll. 35–36: τὸ δὲ ὄνομα τοῦ βασιλέως *κεκρυμμένον* ἐν τοῖς ἔθνεσι· | The name of the emperor is *hidden* from the nations. – *ApcLeonConst* §15, ll. 417–418: τότε ἀναστήσεται σκῆπτρον ἅγιον ἰσχυρὸν *κεκρυμμένον*, [...] | Then a holy, strong, *hidden* scepter will arise, [...]. Cf. *ApcLeonConst* §12, ll. 370–394.

172 *UltVisDan I*, §§49–51 – *VisDanSepCol I*, §2.5–9 – *IntrpGenSch* ll. 38–47.

173 *DiegDan* §5.3: καὶ γενήσεται ἦχος ἐκ τῶν οὐρανῶν μέγας καὶ *σεισμὸς* ἐκ τῆς γῆς φοβερὸς [...] | And there will be a great noise from the heavens and a fearful *earthquake* from the earth [...] – *VisDanSepCol I*, §2.5: τότε *σεισμὸς* γενήσεται, καὶ ὁ λέων πτωχὸς ἐμφανισθήσεται [...] | Then an *earthquake* will occur, and the poor lion will appear [...]. – Cf. Mt 28:2. On the biblical usage of earthquakes, particularly in *Revelation*, see Bauckham 1977. For early and middle Byzantine views on earthquakes, see Dagron 1981. For a cursory discussion of earthquakes in the Byzantine apocalyptic tradition, see Kraft 2021b, pp. 164–166.

been introduced by the *Apocalypse of Ps-Methodios*, where the Savior-Emperor ascends Mount Calvary (Golgotha) in Jerusalem to hand over the imperial insignia—cross and crown—to God in a symbolic act of obliged subordination (*ApcMeth I–III*, 14.2–6). Thereupon, the imperial incumbent passes away in direct reference to the Gospel accounts of Christ's death on the cross.[174] Byzantine apocalyptica thus present the Savior-Emperor as a new martyr.[175] The image of an abdicating and self-sacrificing emperor became another shorthand expression of the messianic end-time ruler.

A third key element of the Savior-Emperor's text-block is the notion of triumph over God's enemies. Given Christ's largely apolitical stance in the Gospels, biblical exegetes had to look to the Old Testament to find material on divine military interventions. A recurring element in Byzantine apocalyptica draws on Ps 77:65 (LXX), where God is compared to a mighty warrior who had previously lain dormant. Apocalyptists drew on this Psalm to combine the hope for sudden redemption with the vision of an invincible warrior. They reinterpreted the verse, replacing God with the Savior-Emperor as the grammatical subject.[176] In so doing, they transferred the mantle of invincibility to God's typological antitype, the Savior-Emperor.

---

174 *ApcMeth I*, 14.6: καὶ ἅμα ὑψωθήσεται ὁ σταυρὸς εἰς τὸν οὐρανόν, καὶ *παραδώσει τὸ πνεῦμα αὐτοῦ* ὁ τῶν Ῥωμαίων βασιλεύς· | And as soon as the cross is lifted into heaven, the king of the Romans *will give up his ghost*. – *ApcAndr* ll. 3919–20: *Παραδώσει* δὲ κυρίῳ τῷ θεῷ σὺν τούτοις καὶ *τὴν ψυχὴν αὐτοῦ.* | Together with them [i.e., the imperial regalia] *he will* also *give up his soul* to the Lord God. – *VisDanSanHom* ll. 528–530: [...] καὶ σὺν αὐτοῖς *παραδώσει* ὁ βασιλεὺς καὶ *τὴν ψυχὴν αὐτοῦ εἰς χεῖρας Θεοῦ αὐτοῦ·* | [...] and together with them [i.e., the imperial regalia] the king *will* also *give up his soul into the hands of his God.* – Cf. Mt 27:50: ὁ δὲ Ἰησοῦς πάλιν κράξας φωνῇ μεγάλῃ *ἀφῆκεν τὸ πνεῦμα.* | Jesus, when he had cried again with a loud voice, *yielded up the ghost.* – Mk 15:37: ὁ δὲ Ἰησοῦς ἀφεὶς φωνὴν μεγάλην *ἐξέπνευσεν.* | And Jesus cried with a loud voice, and *gave up the ghost.* – Lk 23:46: καὶ φωνήσας φωνῇ μεγάλῃ ὁ Ἰησοῦς εἶπεν· Πάτερ, *εἰς χεῖράς σου παρατίθεμαι τὸ πνεῦμά μου*, τοῦτο δὲ εἰπὼν ἐξέπνευσεν. | And when Jesus had cried with a loud voice, he said, Father, *into thy hands I commend my spirit:* and having said thus, he gave up the ghost. – Jn 19:30 [...] καὶ κλίνας τὴν κεφαλὴν *παρέδωκεν τὸ πνεῦμα.* | [...] and he bowed his head, and *gave up the ghost.*

175 On martyrdom as the ideal form of Christomimesis in early Christianity, see Bennema 2025, pp. 323–341.

176 *ApcMeth I*, 13.11: καὶ *ἐξυπνισθήσεται καθάπερ ἄνθρωπος ἀπὸ ὕπνου πιὼν οἶνον πολύν*, [...] | and *he will awake like a man from sleep after drinking much wine*, [...] – *AnonymVatic* p. 49, ll. 23–24: ἀναστήσεται δὲ *ὡς ἐξ ὕπνου καὶ οἴνου κραιπαλικός* [...] | he will rise *as if from sleep and drunk from wine* [...] – *OracLeon* p. 82, l. 4 (Orac. 13): *ὡς ἐκ μέθης* δὲ φανεὶς ἀθρόως· | He appeared suddenly *as if from drunkenness.* – Cf. Ps 77:65 (LXX): καὶ ἐξηγέρθη ὡς ὁ ὑπνῶν κύριος, ὡς δυνατὸς κεκραιπαληκὼς *ἐξ οἴνου*, [...] | Then the Lord awaked as one out of sleep, and like a mighty man that shouteth *by reason of wine.*

In a similar way, Byzantine apocalyptica reinterpreted the original meaning of Dt 32:30 in order to weave further military aspects into the Christomimetic text-block of the Savior-Emperor. Dt 32:30 forms part of the Song of Moses, which gives an account of the circular history of Israel: the privileged treatment by God was ruptured by Israel's unfaithfulness, which triggered divine retribution before culminating in the promise of ultimate redemption. Verse 30 declares that the Israelites' military defeats were not due to their enemies' strength but due to their own weakness, which was the result of God having abandoned them because of their transgressions. Only God's intervention can explain the oddity that a few intruders managed to defeat a multitude.[177] Byzantine political prophecies reinterpreted the verse and reversed its meaning. The original context signified that a handful of external enemies defeated the multitude of the elect. The new meaning was that the elect, who now formed the minority, would defeat a multitude of enemies. The enemy's defeat is spearheaded by the Savior-Emperor, who single-handedly overpowers a host of armed forces, which largely outnumbers his own.[178] The semantic reversal adapts the Deuteronomic motif to the middle Byzantine context, when the New Israel was surrounded by adversarial powers and political redemption was expected to be transacted by a typologically modeled emperor who not only emulates Christ's meekness and self-sacrifice but also fulfills God's commitment to ensure the prosperity of His Chosen People.[179]

Two middle Byzantine apocalypses well illustrate the Savior-Emperor's typological connection to Old Testament models. The *Prophecy of Daniel* and the *Anonymous Prediction* both advance clear but coded references that identify mes-

177 Dt 32:30: *πῶς διώξεται εἷς χιλίους καὶ δύο μετακινήσουσι μυριάδας*, εἰ μὴ ὁ θεὸς ἀπέδοτο αὐτοὺς καὶ κύριος παρέδωκεν αὐτούς; | *How will one pursue a thousand, and two rout ten thousand,* unless God sold them and the Lord surrendered them? (emphasis and translation mine)

178 *ApcMeth I*, 13.10: Τότε πληρωθήσεται τὸ γεγραμμένον· *'εἷς διώξεται χιλίους καὶ δύο μετακινήσουσι μυριάδας'*. | Then will be fulfilled what is written: *'One will pursue a thousand, and two rout ten thousand?'* – *DiegDan* §6.7–8: πληρωθήσεται γὰρ ὁ λόγος ὁ προφητικὸς ὅτι *πῶς διώξεται ὁ εἷς χιλίους καὶ οἱ δύο μετακινήσουσιν μυριάδας* εἰ μὴ ὁ θεὸς ἀπωσάτο αὐτοὺς καὶ ὁ κύριος παρέδωκεν αὐτούς. | Then the prophetic speech will be fulfilled that [says]: *'How will one pursue a thousand, and two rout ten thousand* unless God rejected them and the Lord surrendered them.' – *DiegDan* §5.16: καὶ *διώξει ὁ βασιλεὺς μόνος χιλίους καὶ τὰ δύο μειράκια μυριάδας.* | And *the king alone will pursue a thousand, and the two youths ten thousand.* – *VisDanSepCol I*, §2.14–15: καὶ διώξουσι τοὺς Ἰσμαηλίτας. καὶ πληρωθήσεται ἡ προφητεία ἡ λέγουσα· *εἷς διώξεται χιλίους, καὶ δύο μετακινήσουσι μυριάδας.* | And they will pursue the Ishmaelites, and the prophecy will be fulfilled that says: *one will pursue a thousand, and two will rout ten thousand.*

179 Military concerns dominate political prophecies. Yet, on occasion, the Savior-Emperor is also characterized as a New Moses (e.g., *NarrMend* ll. 19–20), highlighting the perceived need for a new lawgiver.

sianic emperors with a New Phinehas and a New Melchizedek, respectively. The *Prophecy of Daniel* belongs to a group of Sicilian prophecies that originated in the ninth century.[180] It contains an episode in which a savior figure kills an unspecified victim with a "barbed lance".[181] The term "barbed lance" (σιρομάστης) is a rare word and unambiguously evokes Nm 25:7. Nm 25 recounts how the High Priest Phinehas killed in cold blood an Israelite man and his Arab concubine out of religious zeal (ζῆλος). His intention was to halt sexual immorality and idolatry among the Israelites. The biblical account clarifies that God praised Phinehas for his action and awarded him "a perpetual covenant of priesthood".[182] The Church Fathers saw in Phinehas' zeal (and priesthood) a prefiguration of Christ.[183] Accordingly, by assigning the key term "barbed lance" to the savior figure, the *Prophecy of Daniel* establishes a dual connection, casting him in the typology of a New Phinehas while simultaneously likening him to Christ. Like Phinehas, the savior figure is extolled for his violent yet righteous murder; his people (ὁ λαὸς αὐτοῦ) hail him as their sojourning community (παροικία, cf. 1 Pt 1:17).[184] The New Phinehas type also appears prominently in the introduction to the canons

---

180 The text group was identified and dated by Alexander 1985, pp. 62–95. The group consists of four texts: *Slavonic Daniel* (CAVT 265), the *Vision of Daniel by Ps-Chrysostom* (*Ps-Chrys*), the *Vision of Daniel on the Last Times* (*VisioDan*), and the *Prophecy of Daniel* (*ExposDan I*). The last text was unknown to P. Alexander.

181 The episode in question reads as follows: σταθήσεται δὲ ῥίζα [*lege* ῥῆξ] [ἐν] πύλῃ σιδηρᾷ· καὶ ἀναγνῷ γράμματά τινα· καὶ ὁ *σιρομάστης* ὁ ὢν ἐν τῇ χειρὶ αὐτοῦ, εἰσέλθῃ εἰς τὴν καρδίαν αὐτοῦ· καὶ λιποτακτήσει ἐν τῷ αὐτῷ τόπῳ· καὶ ὁ λαὸς αὐτοῦ ἐρεῖ· ἰδού, ἡ παροικία ἡμῶν. | But a king (rēx) will stand at the iron gate and will read certain letters, and the *barbed lance*, which is in his hand, will enter into his heart, and he will defect at that very place. And his people will say: behold, our sojourn! (emphasis mine) – The passage in question is corrupt in all known manuscript witnesses. The cited text has been transcribed (and normalized) from cod. Atheniensis 2187, fol. 2v, saec. XV^{EX}, as the key term σιρομάστης is missing from D. Sakel's edition in *ExposDan I* p. 674, ll. 4–6. The term also appears in the *Vision of Daniel on the Last Times* (*VisioDan*), although in the corrupt form "συνομάστη", which Alexander 1985, pp. 79–80 correctly emended to σιρομάστης. The Athenian manuscript witness now proves Alexander's emendation. Both the *Vision of Daniel on the Last Times* and the *Prophecy of Daniel* are corrupt at various places and would benefit from a synoptic critical edition.

182 Nm 25:13: διαθήκη ἱερατείας αἰωνία.

183 Origenes, *Hom. Num. XX* §5 (pp. 52–54). As one might expect, Origen allegorizes Phinehas' physical violence, contending that Phinehas' act of purification should be emulated in a spiritual manner. For commentary, see Caspary 1979, pp. 34–39.

184 It is negligible in this context whether the historical interpretation by Alexander 1985, pp. 79–83 is correct or not. He argued that the episode presents Emperor Basil I (r. 867–886) as the New Phineas, thereby exonerating Basil for his murder of Michael III in 867, who—according to the typology—was a fornicating idolater. A different historical interpretation has been offered by von Falkenhausen 2023.

of the *Council in Trullo* (692), where Justinian II (r. 685 – 695, 705 – 711) applied the typology to himself.[185] Evidently, the need for a new zealot—one who would reform the New Israelites' morality and vanquish the Arabs— typified the apprehensive atmosphere of the middle Byzantine period.[186]

Another passage that epitomizes the typological frame of reference is contained in the *Anonymous Prediction.* This prophecy, too, appears to have been written in the ninth century. It describes the miraculous appearance of a Savior-Emperor in the following words: "[...] and suddenly a righteous king will rise up, *made like unto the Son of God*, [...]".[187] This short proclamation does not only evoke Christ's sudden and miraculous resurrection but also points to Christ's priestly role as a New Melchizedek. The Byzantine prophecy quotes Heb 7:3, where the Old Testament priest Melchizedek is said to "have neither beginning of days, nor end of life, but *made like unto the Son of God*", signifying everlasting and Christ-like priesthood.[188] The biblical verses that follow present Christ as a New Melchizedek, that is, as the genuinely eternal priest, who is not bound to Levitical descent and is unaffected by either sin or death. Christ's eternal priesthood qualifies Him as a New Melchizedek, just as His zeal qualifies Him as a New Phinehas. The use of Heb 7:3 in the *Anonymous Prediction* denotes that the priestly function of a New Melchizedek is extended to the Savior-Emperor.[189] Due to his Christomimetic character and mission, the Savior-Emperor functions as a New Melchizedek. More generally, the brief prophetic proclamation encapsulates the transitive nature of typological reasoning. Accordingly, if Melchizedek (A) is the typological precursor of Christ (B), and Christ (B) is the typological precursor of the Savior-Emperor (C), then Melchizedek (A) is also the typological precursor of the Savior-Emperor (C). Hence, typological correspondences can manifest them-

185 *Quinisext.* p. 19, ll. 5 – 6 (*Logos prosphōnētikos*). See further Humphreys 2015, pp. 51 – 52, Magdalino 2017, p. 583, and Brandes 2024, pp. 203 – 205. Previously, George of Pisidia had used the typology in reference to Emperor Herakleios, see Georgius Pisides, *In Heracl.* ll. 56 – 58.

186 The typology continued to be used. For an example from the Palaeologan period, see Samara 2018, p. 251, ll. 19 – 24.

187 *AnonymVatic* p. 48, ll. 27 – 28: καὶ ἐξαναστήσεται αἰφνιδίως (cod. εὐνίδιος) βασιλεὺς δίκαιος *ἀφωμοιωμένος τῷ υἱῷ τοῦ θεοῦ* [...].

188 Heb 7:3: ἀπάτωρ ἀμήτωρ ἀγενεαλόγητος, μήτε ἀρχὴν ἡμερῶν μήτε ζωῆς τέλος ἔχων, *ἀφωμοιωμένος δὲ τῷ υἱῷ τοῦ θεοῦ*, μένει ἱερεὺς εἰς τὸ διηνεκές. | Without father, without mother, without descent, *having neither beginning of days, nor end of life; but made like unto the Son of God*; abideth a priest continually. (emphasis added) – On the Melchizedek typology in the New Testament, see Goppelt 1966, pp. 196 – 205.

189 It should be noted that the *Anonymous Prediction* presents the Savior-Emperor not only as the New Melchizedek but also as the New Joshua (son of Nun), see *AnonymVatic* p. 49, ll. 2 – 7. The former typology carries more profound implications and thus warrants closer scrutiny.

selves in multiple instantiations. The following instantiations of the Christ-type are given by the *Anonymous Prediction* and its immediate manuscript environment (Figure 1).

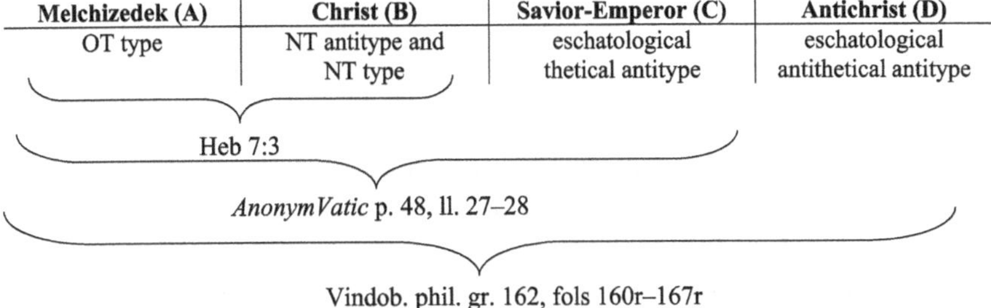

Figure 1: Typological model of the Christ-type.

The diagram shows how the typology begins with Melchizedek as the thetical (or positive) precursor of Christ, who, in turn, serves as the thetical type of the Savior-Emperor. The biblical typology of Heb 7 is readily projected into the impending future. But the sequence does not end there. It continues and culminates in the figure of the Antichrist. It should be noted that, strictly speaking, the Antichrist motif does not appear in the *Anonymous Prediction* but in the immediate manuscript context. The *Anonymous prediction* ends abruptly in the middle of folio 163v in cod. Vindobonensis phil. gr. 162, saec. XV[1], which is the *codex unicus* of the prophecy.[190] The abrupt end is hard to discern, given that the text transitions to the next prophecy, the *Last Vision of Daniel*, without any indication. The manuscript suggests a continuous text. Without knowing that the *Last Vision of Daniel* constitutes a separate text in most other manuscripts, the reader would fail to realize that the *Anonymous Prediction* ends half way through the folio and would go on reading. As a result, the reader would conflate the Antichrist motif, contained

190 While the *Anonymous Prediction* is preserved in a single manuscript, the Melchizedek typology reappears in the *Tale of the True Emperor*, at *NarrMend* ll. 62–64. This probably thirteenth-century pastiche of apocalyptic text-blocks is known to be contained in at least 40 manuscripts. For an overview of the manuscript tradition, see Kraft 2018a, pp. 113–114. To the list should now be added: codd. Atheniensis 2501, fols 276v–277r, ann. 1626 and Atheniensis Universitatis Bibliothēkēs tēs Philosophikēs Scholēs 14, fols 242v–243r, saec. XVII. For a general discussion of the text, see Alexander 1985, pp. 130–136 and Brandes 2013. See further Mesler 2007, who has shown that the earliest textual evidence for this prophecy is its Latin translation, which was produced around 1330 in Italy.

at the end of the *Last Vision of Daniel*, with the Melchizedek typology from the *Anonymous prediction*.

The identification of the Savior-Emperor with a New Melchizedek is based on a longstanding and contested tradition that viewed Melchizedek not only as the type of Christ but also of the Christian Roman emperor. However, this connection was typically inferred rather than stated explicitly.[191] The sanctuary mosaics of San Vitale in Ravenna are a good case in point, for they pictorially fuse emperor and priest without making the claim seem exceedingly blunt and conceited. This mid-sixth-century mosaic program famously depicts Emperor Justinian (r. 527–565) in imperial garb holding the paten for the Eucharistic host, thereby indicating his priestly function. To corroborate the emperor's priesthood, the mosaic program shows Melchizedek on the opposite wall, dressed as an emperor and holding the sacrificial bread in an offertory gesture.[192] The basis of Melchizedek's sacrificial role is Gn 14:18, where he offers bread to Abraham, which was generally understood as the typological prefiguration of the Eucharist.[193] Gn 14:18 and Heb 7:1 specify that Melchizedek is both king and priest. The San Vitale mosaic program shows Melchizedek—as well as Justinian—in this dual function. Both are presented in their priestly and kingly duties. Another notable depiction of Melchizedek as the typological precursor of the priestly emperor is the manuscript illumination of the *Christian Topography* by Kosmas Indikopleustēs in cod. Vaticanus gr. 699, fol. 58r, saec. IX. Here, Melchizedek is depicted as a Byzantine emperor, wearing the imperial crown and cloak (purple *chlamys* with a golden *tablion*), and as a

191 It is disputed whether Eusebios was the first to honor a Christian emperor with the role of a New Melchizedek, as suggested by Rapp 2010, p. 193. The New Melchizdek typology appears in Eusebios' panegyric to Paulinus, which he later integrated into his *Church History*, see Eusebius, *Hist. eccl.* 10.4.23 (pp. 869–870). The title of the panegyric identifies the addressee with Paulinus, Bishop of Tyre, whom Schott 2011, pp. 189–190 and Corke-Webster 2019, pp. 54–56 consider the focus of the praise. In contrast, Rapp 2010 has proposed to identify the addressee with Emperor Constantine, who may have been present when the oration was delivered. However, dating the oration to c. 315 AD (Barnes 1981, p. 162) excludes Constantine's presence. Still, one may wonder whether Eusebios had not only Paulinus in mind but also the co-emperors Constantine (r. 306–337) and Licinius (r. 308–324), who enabled the peace and prosperity that the oration celebrates. Even if this were the case, Eusebios refrained from explicitly identifying Constantine as the New Melchizedek. This position aligns with a general reluctance in Byzantium to do so as well as with Eusebios' other writings, which assign Constantine a quasi-priestly role *outside* the Church. For discussion and references, see Dagron 1996, pp. 145–148.

192 See Leach 1972, pp. 11–12, Dillenberger 1986, p. 30, Homan 2006, pp. 32–34, and Jensen 2019, pp. 601–606. The mosaics can be viewed online under: https://projects.mcah.columbia.edu/ha/panos/San-Vitale/Apse (last accessed: 1/1/2026).

193 For references, see Grypeou and Spurling 2013, pp. 225–226.

priest, standing in supplicatory pose and distinguished by the golden halo of a saintly figure.[194]

Notwithstanding the recurrent use of the Melchizedek typology,[195] the emperor's priestly aspirations did not go unchallenged. Maximos the Confessor openly opposed the emperor's priestly ambitions. According to the record of his trial in 655, Maximos forcefully rejected the emperor's meddling in doctrinal affairs, asserting that the inquiry into and definition of Church teaching is the prerogative of priests, not of emperors.[196] When prompted about the emperor's priestly authority, Maximos countered that he is not a priest, as proven by his different dress and the fact that he does not officiate the sacraments. More importantly, he rejected outright the typological equation of the emperor with Melchizedek. According to Maximos, Melchizedek's antitype can only be Christ, since He alone is *by nature* (φύσει) both king and priest as well as without beginning and end (Heb 7:3). Maximos is quoted to have said: "Melchizedek was a unique prefiguration."[197] That is to say, he rejected the repeated instantiation of that typology. Christ is the only antitype of this specific *typos*. To say otherwise would entail idolatry by assuming another eternal ('without beginning and end') deity who has become man.[198] Maximos challenged the imperial custom to claim sacerdotal privileges by applying an unusually literal exegesis that requires the New Melchizedek to be *by nature* 'without beginning and end'. He precluded the possibility that a New Melchizedek could be an emperor whose genealogy was merely unknown or uncertain, similarly to the unknown origin of Melchizedek himself. As pointed out above, a common element in the Savior-Emperor text-block was the notion of hiddenness, which is semantically akin to an unknown origin. Maximos' hardliner attitude held that the emperor could not even in principle function as the typological continuation of Melchizedek. By extension, his skepticism called into question whether the emperor could be a forerunner of the returning Christ at all. Essen-

194 The image is discussed by Dagron 1996, pp. 188–190. It is accessible online under: https://digi.vatlib.it/view/MSS_Vat.gr.699 (last accessed: 1/1/2026). For a discussion of Kosmas' epistemology and ideology, which inform the *Christian Topography*, see MacCormack 1982.

195 On Melchizedek in the fourteenth-century murals of the Chōra monastery, see Kotoula (forthcoming). For additional references to historical sources and scholarly discussions of the Melchizedek motif, see von Erffa 1995, pp. 59–76.

196 Maximus Confessoris, *Rel. mot.* pp. 25–27 (ll. 177–206). Translation by Allen and Neil 2002, pp. 57–59. The importance of this passage was highlighted by Dagron 1996, pp. 179–184. For the historical context of the trial and the perspective of the trial record, see Neil 2006 and Louth 2017.

197 Maximus Confessoris, *Rel. mot.* p. 27, l. 193: […] εἷς ὑπῆρχεν τύπος ὁ Μελχισεδέκ.

198 Maximus Confessoris, *Rel. mot.* p. 27, ll. 197–198: ἄλλος γὰρ εὑρεθήσεται Θεὸς ὁ τοιοῦτος ἐνανθρωπήσας […]

tially, what Maximos denied was the emperor's fitness for typological instantiation.[199]

The trial record states that Maximos' contentious refutation was triggered by a dignitary's outspoken assertion that the emperor was a New Melchizedek. He is shown to have merely reacted to an ostentatious arrogation. The explicit and hence pretentious claim to be both emperor and priest was suspect to many Byzantines, as such boastful behavior was deemed unbefitting the emperor's Christomimetic humility and meekness. Gilbert Dagron, in his masterful discussion of the Melchizedek typology in Byzantium, highlighted a fundamental paradox: one could claim the typology only indirectly by means of allusions and subtle references. Any explicit vindication thereof was seen to invalidate the very claim.[200] Dagron noted that an explicit claim would have been construed as boastful behavior and viewed with suspicion, as it resembled the expected conduct of the Antichrist. For context, Dagron pointed to the apocalyptic script of the *Apocalypse of Leo of Constantinople*, in which a saintly monk opposes an ostentatious and wicked emperor.[201] Further examples could be given, which all express the apprehensiveness about the emperor's potential to become the Antichrist (or one of his precursors).[202] Various emperors—including Constantius II (r. 337–361), Justinian I (r. 527–565), Nikephoros I (r. 802–811), and Andronikos I (r. 1183–1185)—were suspected by their contemporaries to have fallen into this role.[203] Likewise, Commentaries on *Revelation* reflect the widespread anxiety that the Antichrist would rule as emperor.[204] It is in this context that the typolog-

199 Maximos' rebuttal of the imperial use of the Melchizedek typology was thus little short of treason, which explains the harsh punishment he was subjected to. It is no coincidence that followers of Maximos were among the first to identify Constantinople with the Great Whore of Babylon (Rv 17–18), expressing their disapproval with imperial policies in the harshest possible terms; see Anonymus, *Contr. Const.* pp. 231–232, cf. Rv 17:6. On the dating and significance of the text, see Bracke 1980, pp. 174–178 and Brandes 2003, pp. 62, 69.
200 Dagron 1996, pp. 169–200, at 190.
201 Dagron 1996, pp. 182, 200, presumably having in mind the first half of the narrative: *ApcLeonConst* §§4–13, ll. 84–401. The first part of the apocalypse climaxes when the wicked emperor mocks his opponents (i.e., saintly monks) and boasts about being the savior, see *ApcLeonConst* §13, ll. 395–399: Ὁ δὲ παράνομος βασιλεύς [...] καθίσας ἐπὶ θρόνου αὐτοῦ [...] ἐπερωτᾷ· 'ἔχουσι θεὸν οἱ ἀββάδες; οὐχὶ ἐγὼ ἐλευθερώσω τὸν κόσμον;' | But the lawless king [...] sitting on his throne [...] asks: 'Do the fathers have a god? Will it not be me who liberates the world?'
202 *ApcMeth I–III*, 14.10 – *Ps-Chrys* §6.8 – *DiegDan* §13.1–10. Cf. *ApcAndr* ll. 3982–86 – *UltVisDan I*, §§66–68, where a wicked woman boasts and taunts God.
203 See Flower 2019 (Constantius II), Rubin 1951, Meier 2003, pp. 86–89, Denson 2022 (Justinian I), Torgerson 2022, pp. 272–313 (Nikephoros I), and Kraft 2024 (Andronikos I).
204 See above note 62.

ical sequence shown in the diagram above needs to be understood. The Antichrist was expected to continue and pervert the Christomimetic typology.

The Antichrist is the ultimate antagonist in Christian eschatology. The main sources of the Antichrist motif were the canonical works of the Johannine and Pauline epistles as well as *Revelation.*[205] Patristic writings, such as Hippolytos' discourse *On Christ and the Antichrist* and various homilies from the Ephraem Graecus corpus, provide the secondary foundation for the Antichrist myth in Byzantium.[206] Following 2 Thes 2:6–7, the Antichrist was generally believed to appear only after the "withholding force" (τὸ κατέχον/ὁ κατέχων) had been removed.[207] Byzantine political ideology identified this withholding force with Roman power.[208] Accordingly, the Antichrist would only arrive once the Roman Empire had been removed, making him the last political actor prior to Christ's Second Coming. This conviction corresponded to the forementioned exegesis that identified the fourth Danielic kingdom with the Christian Roman Empire.[209] The Antichrist was thus believed to usurp Roman political power and to establish a perverted form of monarchic rule.[210]

Byzantine prophecies expected the Antichrist to perform a variety of "marvelous and astonishing deeds" in order to deceive Jews and Christians alike.[211] Those marvelous deeds encompassed some of the very miracles that Christ had performed. The descriptions of those pseudo-miracles are fashioned after the Gospel accounts and include, most commonly, the healing of the blind, lame, and deaf.[212] There existed a range of typological options concerning which other miracles the Antichrist could be credited with. None of the prophecies surveyed here

---

205 1 Jn 2:18–22, 4:2–3, and 2 Jn 7 as well as 2 Thes 2:1–12. The passages from Mt 24:24 and Mk 13:22 have generally been taken to refer to the Antichrist as well. Moreover, one of two beasts of Rv 13 was understood to represent the Antichrist. For possible identifications, see Andreas Caesariensis, *In Apoc.* cap. 36–37 (pp. 135–144) (comm. on Rv 13:1–17).

206 Among the numerous writings of the Ephraem Graecus corpus, the *Sermon on the Second Coming of Christ* (CPG 3940) is of particular relevance. Edition in Phrantzolas 1992, pp. 111–128. For a useful introduction to the corpus and a targeted discussion of the homily, see Grypeou 2013.

207 For an analysis of the historical context of the Pauline motif, see Betz 1963 and Metzger 2005.

208 For references, see Podskalsky 1972, p. 55.

209 See above note 66.

210 On the incipient development of the Antichrist legend, see the still foundational work by Bousset 1895. See further Jenks 1991, Lietaert Peerbolte 1996, and McGinn 2000, pp. 33–78. On the Antichrist in Byzantium, see Podskalsky 1972, pp. 86–91, *passim* and Alexander 1985, pp. 193–225.

211 *UltVisDan I*, §74: καὶ οὕτως βασιλεύσει ὁ ἀντίχριστος καὶ πράξει θαυμαστὰ καὶ παράδοξα πράγματα. | And thus the Antichrist will reign and perform marvelous and astonishing deeds.

212 *ApcMeth I–III*, 14.8 – *Ps-Chrys* §6.5 – *VisioDan* §5.11 – *VisDanSanHom* ll. 685–686. These passages quote Mt 11:5, Lk 7:22, thereby casting the Antichrist's false miracle-workings as a perverted inversion of Christ's healings.

mention any attempt by the Antichrist to resurrect the dead. Byzantine apocalyptica seem to argue *ex silentio* that the Antichrist could not repeat this miracle.[213] Some apocalyptic texts related the expectation that he would reenact Christ's walking on water (Mt 14:25, Mk 6:48, Jn 6:19), while others anticipated that he would imitate Christ's voice.[214]

The *Diegesis of Daniel* transmits a rare tradition of the Antichrist as someone who attempts to transform stone into bread. The attempt fails. Instead of turning into bread, the stone transforms into a dragon, who denounces the Antichrist for trickery and lawlessness.[215] Although the exact provenance of this story is unclear, it reverberates with the language of the Gospels with regard to Christ's healing miracles (Mk 2:11).[216] Moreover, it inverts Christ's first temptation, when the devil challenged him to perform this very miracle in the desert (Mt 4:3, Lk 4:3).[217] In contrast to Christ, the Antichrist attempts to perform this miracle.[218] The very attempt shows his haughtiness, which disqualifies him from accomplishing the feat. Again, boastful behavior was considered a hallmark of the Antichrist.

As pointed out above, the Antichrist was generally expected to be a Roman emperor. That is why, any boastful behavior by a monarch was potent in invoking the suspicion that he was a typological precursor of the Antichrist, if not the Antichrist himself. Byzantine apocalyptica underscore the semantic overlap of the Antichrist and emperor with various statements that are asserted for the former

213 One possible exception is Andreas Caesariensis, *In Apoc.* cap. 36 (p. 138) (comm. on Rv 13:4), where the Antichrist is explicitly credited with the resurrection of the dead. See further Bousset 1895, pp. 116–119. However, this text is not a prophecy but a biblical commentary.

214 Walking on water: Hippolytus (Ps-), *De consum.* §26, ll. 11–12 – *ApcLeonConst* §19, ll. 520–525. Imitation of Christ's voice: Romanus Melodus, *Hymn.* 50, §11 (p. 248, l. 13): τούτου γὰρ μιμεῖται τὴν φωνὴν […] – *ApcLeonConst* §18, ll. 502–503: μιμούμενος τοῦ Μεσία τὴν φωνήν. According to Hippolytus (Ps-), *De consum.* §20, the Antichrist will also imitate Christ in being like a lion, king, and lamb.

215 *DiegDan* §13.9–14. The motif appears first in the *Seventh Vision of Daniel*, a late fifth-century Byzantine prophecy that has survived only in Armenian translation. See *SepVisDan* p. 134, l. 3: ի քարանց հաց հանել | to extract bread from stones. – For alternative translations, see Issaverdens 1901, p. 345 and La Porta 2013, p. 433 (§37.5). The motif also appears in *ApcLeonConst* §19, ll. 516–520.

216 Cf. Mk 5:41, Lk 5:24, Lk 7:14. See further Berger 1976, p. 141.

217 For the typological significance of this motif within the *Gospel of Matthew*, see Daniélou 1950, p. 136.

218 There is an additional layer in this typology, which associates the Antichrist's failed miracle with Moses' miracle of producing water "from a flinty rock" (ἐκ πέτρας ἀκροτόμου, Dt 8:15) while wandering in the wilderness. The same expression is used in *DiegDan* §13.11: σοὶ λέγω τῇ ἀκροτόμῳ πέτρᾳ· γένου ἄρτος ἐνώπιον τῶν Ἰουδαίων. | I say to you, flinty rock: become bread before the Jews. – The Antichrist is thus presented as a false Christ and a false Moses.

but denied for the latter. For instance, the Antichrist is said to be "dead and useful for nothing", while the very same characterization is rebutted for the Savior-Emperor.[219] A similar contrast appears in the juxtaposition of the genuine prosperity that the Savior-Emperor brings about with the merely ephemeral prosperity provided by the Antichrist.[220] These passages show that it was the duty of the emperor to ensure affluence and to prove his worth. The Antichrist, being a fraudulent king, fails to meet those standards. Therefore, Byzantine apocalypses constructed the *Anti*-Christ not only as the typological foil for Christ but also the Savior-Emperor. The adjacency of the Savior-Emperor and Antichrist in the apocalyptic script, semantic overlaps, the transitive nature of typological reasoning, and the political nature of the prophecies under scrutiny all reaffirm the Christocentric typology that posits the Savior-Emperor and the Antichrist as instantiations—thetical and antithetical—of the Christ-type.[221]

These examples should suffice to demonstrate that Byzantine apocalyptica revolve around typologically informed motifs. When weaving the fabric of providential history, Byzantine apocalyptists used typological constructs that reverberated with past events of salvation history—first and foremost Christological events—in order to contextualize and interpret contemporary and anticipated events. Typological correspondences were the warp onto which the stock motifs of the apocalyptic script were woven and from which the textual tapestry of apocalyptic history gained its structure.

---

219 See *ApcMeth I*, 14.11: Παρουσίᾳ οὖν πάντων τῶν ἐθνῶν ἐλέγξουσιν αὐτοῦ τὴν πλάνην καὶ ἀναδείξουσιν αὐτὸν [scil. τὸν υἱὸν τῆς ἀπωλείας] ψεύστην ἐπὶ παντὸς ἀνθρώπου καὶ *μηδὲν ὄντα* [...] | In the presence of all nations they will reveal his deceit, and they will show him [i.e., the son of perdition] to be a liar upon all man and *to be nothing* [...]. – The passage should be read together with *ApcMeth I*, 13.11 [...] ὃν [scil. τὸν βασιλέα Ῥωμαίων] ἐλογίζοντο οἱ ἄνθρωποι ὡσεὶ νεκρὸν ὄντα καὶ εἰς *οὐδὲν χρησιμεύοντα*· | [...] whom [i.e., the Roman emperor] people were considering to be dead and *good for nothing*. – The contrast is repeated in *VisioDan* §5.16 (Antichrist), §2.5 (Savior-Emperor).

220 Compare *DiegDan* §6.24 with *DiegDan* §11.36–37, §12.6, where sustainable prosperity is contrasted to short-lived and, hence, false abundance.

221 The emperor's ambivalence—being either sacred or wicked—is visually epitomized in the *Menologion of Basil II*. Cod. Vaticanus gr. 1613, saec. XI^{IN} contains a deluxe edition of this liturgical book, depicting wicked (Antichrist-like) emperors with blue halos (p. 100: Emperor Julian; pp. 170, 234: Emperor Maximian; p. 281: King Herod) and sacred (Christ-like) emperors with golden ones (p. 108: Emperor Constantine VI; p. 350: Emperor Theodosios II; p. 392: Empress Theodora, wife of Emperor Theophilos). The manuscript can be viewed online under: https://digi.vatlib.it/view/MSS_Vat.gr.1613 (last accessed: 1/1/2026). For the text and English translation of the *Menologion*, see Kuper 2025. I thank Roland Betancourt for having drawn my attention to this manuscript and its color code.

3.3 Typological chronotopes

Typological continuity guaranteed an orderly transition into the post-apocalyptic world, no matter the specific events of the end times. The motifs of a new antediluvian calm, a new Exodus, and new instantiations of Christomimetic deeds and behavior all served to introduce providential order into the avowed upheaval preceding the *eschaton.* Typology was used as a compositional method and hermeneutical approach that applied biblical historiography to the post-testamental period, aligning the present and future with scriptural patterns.

Typologies refer to the past, explain the present, and point towards the future. They draw on the paleo-Christian tension between the already accomplished but not yet fulfilled redemption.[222] Accordingly, typologies select disparate events from salvation history and orient them toward the singular interval of the *eschaton.* The agglomeration of chronologically diverse typologies within the transient eschatological period gives the impression that history is being reduced to its core soteriological events; it is condensed to its constitutive, typological patterns, from which historical redundancies are subtracted. As a result, diachronic history appears to collapse into a unitary culmination that resembles the atemporal divine perspective in which past, present, and future are indistinguishable and singular. In other words, typology not only condenses history, but it also converges upon divine atemporality. Typology neutralizes time.[223]

Put differently, typology injects God's atemporal synchronicity into diachronic history, thereby functioning as an ontological bridge between two temporal dimensions. The typological patterns embody the eternal present of God's providence, while the historical events on which they are mapped constitute worldly diachronicity. Apocalyptists professed to unveil the hidden semantic bridges by identifying the temporal coordinates of disjointed events and characters and by exposing the typological grid beneath them.[224] In a word, typologies transcend diachronic time and are governed by the logic of the eternal present.

---

222 Cullmann 1962, pp. 88, 180, *passim* is renowned for having highlighted this tension.

223 Averintsev 1975, pp. 273–274 observed that typology neutralizes the lapse of time but does not obliterate it.

224 Titles of historical apocalypses indicate that their literary authority is based on the claim of being 'revelations'. The most common designations include 'vision' (ὅρασις), 'oracle' (χρησμός), 'prophecy' (προφητεία), or 'prediction' (πρόφθεγμα). At times, they also use the less revelatory categories of 'narrative' (λόγος), 'narration' (διήγησις), or 'exposition' (ἀπόδειξις). The alternative term 'prognostication' (πρόγνωσις) is usually reserved for technical, scientific forecasts, see Kountoura-Galakē 2001, p. 437. That said, it remains to be studied to what extent these appellations were used interchangeably or whether subtle distinctions were drawn consistently.

The suspension of diachronic time is a chronotopic characteristic of historical apocalyptica. The notion of chronotope was introduced by Mikhail Bakhtin to examine how literary works express spatiotemporal properties.[225] He defined a chronotope as the artistic expression of time and space in literature and assigned it a constitutive function for the definition of a literary genre. Chronotopes are internal patterns of literary works, which are separate from external aspects, such as the transmission or reception history. Originally, Bakhtin used the chronotopic approach to discuss the evolution of the European novel from the Greek romance to Rabelais. But the approach lends itself also to other literary genres, such as apocalypses. Michael Vines applied the chronotopic perspective to the thorny issue of defining apocalypses. He argued—in opposition to Collins' classical approach mentioned above—that apocalypses ought to be defined on the basis of their "meta-linguistic form", which includes the chronotopic characteristic of suspending normal temporal and spatial boundaries.[226] The issue of defining apocalypses does not need to detain us here. What matters for our purposes is the recognition that the Bakhtinian approach can facilitate the analysis of temporal elements in Byzantine apocalyptica.

Following Bakhtin's analysis of the European novel, the chronotope of Byzantine historical apocalypses can be qualified as follows. Apocalyptic time is characterized by random coincidence (случайное совпадение), which is not seldom expressed by the adverb "suddenly" (вдруг), quite similarly to the adventure novel of ordeal.[227] Evidently, behind those coincidences stands divine providence, but the divine purpose does not abolish the ostensibly random and spontaneous appearance of those coincidences. Furthermore, apocalyptic narratives rarely develop characters of protagonists. While figures, such as the Savior-Emperor or Gog and Magog, can be described in vivid detail, they do not mature. Their roles are stagnant, limited strictly to their narrative purpose.[228] Even when individualized

---

225 Bakhtin 1975, pp. 234–407 (translation in Bakhtin 1981, pp. 84–258).

226 Vines 2007, pp. 112–114. He goes on to argue that—in addition to the chronotope of suspending spatiotemporal boundaries—apocalypses share in common the passivity of the apocalyptic hero and a "profoundly monologic" tone. Byzantine apocalyptica provide several examples that could challenge, or at least qualify, the latter view. For instance, the aforementioned prayers and pleas may come to mind, which attribute some dialogic agency to the hero. See above note 80.

227 Bakhtin 1975, p. 242 (Bakhtin 1981, p. 92). Cf. the references to Byzantine apocalypses in note 167 and 176 together with *ApcLeonConst* §10, l. 333, §22, l. 594: εὐθέως | immediately. Suddenness is a common device also in moral apocalypses, e.g., *VisNiph* §§85–87, *passim:* θᾶττον | quickly; ἄφνω | suddenly – *ApcMarVir* §§4–5 (pp. 116–117), *passim:* εὐθέως | immediately.

228 Cf. Bakhtin 1975, p. 261 (Bakhtin 1981, p. 110).

with physical descriptions or onomastic allusions,[229] the hero (or villain) remains a symbolic figure, much like those found in chivalric romances.[230] Another similarity with chivalric romances is the feature that time miraculously compresses or drags out, which is analogous to the apocalyptic motif of the shortening of days.[231] It also resembles the typological protraction of the *synteleia*, to which we will return shortly. Moreover, the narrative sequence of transgression, retribution, redemption, and salvation, which is quintessential to apocalypses, is characteristic also of the adventure novel of everyday life.[232] In other words, Byzantine apocalypses share a chronotope that, in several respects, parallels pre-modern novelistic literature.

A chief chronotopic difference that sets historical apocalyptica apart from pre-modern novels is the irreversibility of time. While novelistic time is generally reversible and interchangeable, apocalyptic time is unidirectional and sequential. Even though certain events could be chronologically rearranged, as shown above in Table 1, the overall narrative schema was invariable, and its trajectory was fixed towards the Antichrist and the Last Judgment. Historical apocalypses are focused on the sequence, duration, and typology of worldly, time-bound events. In contrast, they have little concern for spatial aspects. It is true that the locations of key events are frequently specified by name, but their identity is interchangeable, as they are not essential to the plot. This is confirmed by the fact that toponyms frequently change in the transmission history. By and large, locations are fungible. In short, space can be rearranged, but time cannot be reversed.[233] The chronotope of historical apocalypses is marked by the irreversibility of temporal properties. The ever-escalating trajectory of typology translates into unidirectional temporality.

The chronotopic features of coincidence and spontaneity, symbolic referentiality and stagnant disposition, time compression and sequentiality, a fixed narrative plot and temporal irreversibility are all salient characteristics of historical

---

229 Physiognomy: *ExposDan I*, p. 674, ll. 14–16 – *VisioDan* §2.1–2 – *UltVisDan I*, §47. Name: *ExposDan I*, p. 674, l. 16 – *VisioDan* §2.4 – *DiegDan* §5.7, §6.22 – *VisDanSepCol I*, §2.5.

230 Bakhtin 1975, p. 303 (Bakhtin 1981, p. 153).

231 Bakhtin 1975, pp. 304–305 (Bakhtin 1981, pp. 154–155).

232 Bakhtin 1975, pp. 269–280 (Bakhtin 1981, pp. 118–129).

233 The exact opposite holds true for moral apocalypses. The main concern of moral apocalypses is spatiality. Moral apocalypses explore the otherworldly geography and decode its symbolic significance. The dimension of time is largely relegated to the tension between the timeless simultaneity of otherworldly conditions and the seemingly unceasing suffering of sinners. For further discussion, see the references above in note 3. In this regard, the chronotope of heavenly journeys contrasts with that found in historical apocalypses.

apocalyptica. Most of these features are either informed by or derive directly from typological reasoning. Consequently, typology decisively shapes the chronotope of this apocalyptic subgenre. Bakhtin concluded his analysis by comparing the chronotope to the juncture where "the knots of the narrative are tied and untied".[234] The simile is equally applicable to typology, which functions much like a thread that lines up historical characters like gems on a string.[235] Typology is a chronotopic device.

The typological chronotope of historical prophecies upsets the classical dichotomy of linear and cyclical time. Although historical apocalypses generally proceed in gradual succession, their typological underpinning transcends chronological sequence. Typologies superimpose repetition on progression, merging the cyclical and linear dimensions of time. They incorporate "temporal recapitulation[s]" into diachronic history.[236] For this reason, apocalyptic time has been compared to the geometrical shape of a spiral.[237] Whether one agrees with the utility of spatial metaphors or not, the antithesis between linear and cyclical time is untenable given the hybridization of temporal aspects in apocalyptic narratives.[238] Apocalyptic time is multitemporal, encompassing both sequential (linear) and synchronous (cyclical) aspects.

This duality of the typological chronotope allows for the protraction of the *synteleia* by multiplying instantiations. As shown above, the typological coordinates are not always binary and can be multiple.[239] In particular, Christ-like figures can appear innumerable times, as they do not represent mere historical recurrences but rather express the continuous manifestation of the already realized

234 Bakhtin 1975, p. 398: В хронотопе завязываются и развязываются сюжетные узлы. (Bakhtin 1981, p. 250).
235 Cf. page 57 above.
236 I borrow the term from Leach 1972, pp. 7 10, who talks about typology without explicitly naming the concept. Similarly, Frye 1982, p. 84 considers "typology [] a specialized form of the repeatability of myth". Cf. Gil 1992, who discusses cyclical elements in the Christian tradition, including typology, and maintains that these elements are remnants of pagan influence. This view can be rebutted, given that typologies were already used in the Old Testament. For references, see above note 138.
237 Flannery-Dailey 1999. Similarly, also Keller 1996, p. 88. Cf. Demandt 2015, pp. 18, 21, who uses the analogy of a cart or chariot, whereby the rotation of the wheel illustrates cyclic time, and the forward motion typifies linear time.
238 Cf. Le Goff 1960, p. 430 and Barr 1962, pp. 137–142, who caution against the facile contrast of cyclical (Greek) and linear (Christian) time.
239 Cf. Guinot 1989, pp. 10–11, 21, who points out that declarative, verbal prophecies (διὰ λόγου, διὰ ῥημάτων)—which are to be distinguished from prophecies through historical events (διὰ τύπου, διὰ πραγμάτων)—could be realized more than once, given that an earlier realization was incomplete and, thus, needed subsequent fulfillment.

eschatology achieved through Christ's incarnation and sacrifice.[240] The apposition of the *Anonymous Prediction* with the *Last Vision of Daniel* in the Viennese manuscript provides a pertinent example, where Melchizedek, the Savior-Emperor, and the Antichrist are all typologically linked to Christ by means of the lapidary yet evocative reference to Heb 7:3. Further examples can be found in the alternating sequences of Christ-like and Antichrist-like rulers in the *Apocalypse of Andrew the Fool* and the *Apocalypse of Leo of Constantinople.* The figure of a Christ-like emperor could be repeated indefinitely, either in its thetical or antithetical form. As a result, the set of eschatological tasks, laid out in the *Apocalypse of Ps-Methodios*, could be spread across successive figures.[241] Typologies were inherently open to multiple instantiations and not limited to a pair of counterparts.[242] They could thus be used as yet another means to increase the narrating time and defer the end phenomenologically.

The Christ-typology displays not only the multiplicity but also the axiological multivalency of typological reasoning. As shown above, the Savior-Emperor and Antichrist share much in common. Their role as monarch and their Christ-like characteristics make them hard to distinguish. Byzantine apocalypses never tire of emphasizing the cunning and duplicitous nature of the Antichrist, which makes him virtually unrecognizable by outside factors alone. His wickedness is revealed only gradually, first by his false miracles, then by the two witnesses Enoch and Elijah, and eventually by Christ Himself. The passage of time is thus given an epistemological function. Only through time can his true nature be discovered. Time serves as an epistemic (as well as ontological) substrate in which the supratemporal (anti)types are recognized (and realized) in either their thetical or antithetical form. In sum, multitemporality, multiplicity, and multivalency specify the typological chronotope of Byzantine historical apocalyptica.

---

240 Realized eschatology assumes that the Kingdom of Heaven is already immanent in this world. See Meyendorff 1974, p. 219, Podskalsky 1984, pp. 441–442, and Magdalino 1993, pp. 10–15.
241 See above note 85. E.g., *ApcAndr* ll. 3824–3920 – *UltVisDan I*, §§47–61, where the functions of 1) politically reconstituting the empire and 2) the imperial abdication have been distributed between two successive emperors.
242 The multiplicity of the messiah-typology appears also in the Jewish apocalyptic tradition. On the two messiahs (Messiah ben Joseph and Messiah ben David), see Himmelfarb 2017. See further Ben-Sasson 2024, pp. 618–626 and Ben-Sasson 2026, pp. 106–132, who discusses the appearance of two anti-messiahs in the Hebrew *Vision of Daniel* from the St. Petersburg collection.

4 Conclusion

Современность, взятая вне своего отношения
к прошлому и будущему, утрачивает свое единство,
рассыпается на единичные явления и вещи,
становится абстрактным конгломератом их.[243]
Mikhail Bakhtin

Byzantine apocalyptica articulate a varied yet coherent understanding of apocalyptic time using a range of literary strategies. Chapter One explored the strategies that were used to estimate when the *synteleia* would occur. This was done either directly by computation or indirectly by describing the signs of the end. The result was an apocalyptic script that consisted of a series of stock motifs and a chronological sequence that was both malleable and consistent. Far from being deterministic, the apocalyptic script could be updated and delayed. The resulting textual plasticity informed a metahistory that conditioned the audience's horizon of expectations.[244] Chapter Two investigated the literary techniques by which the texts manipulate the reader's perception of apocalyptic time, both objectively and phenomenologically. Time compression and fluctuations in narrative speed convey a temporal atmosphere that is both accelerated and arrhythmic, akin to ventricular fibrillation, which is indicative of impending heart failure. As in a medical handbook, the reader of historical apocalypses is primed to recognize temporal anomalies as necessary precursors to cosmic collapse. Although acceleration was key, deceleration, too, was symptomatic of the disintegration of cosmic, diachronic time.[245] Apocalyptists made sure to leave enough time to address the immediate needs of their audiences. Gradual changes in the text tradition show that the more the political prospects for imperial recovery declined in late Byzantium, the more the apocalypses deferred the *synteleia* to the rather distant future. Paradoxically, existential crises were prone to delay rather than hasten the *escha-*

243 Bakhtin 1975, p. 296 (Bakhtin 1981, p. 146: If taken outside its relationship to past and future, the present loses its integrity, breaks down into isolated phenomena and objects, making of them a mere abstract conglomeration).
244 The term "metahistory" was shaped by White 1973, who argued that historical accounts are inherently interpretive, dependent on the authors' narrative structures and literary techniques. This observation applies also to historical apocalypses. Accordingly, the meaning of Byzantine (historical) apocalyptica is determined by an overarching understanding of history (metahistory) that relies on a coherent chronology and effective literary techniques (e.g., narrative speed, typological reasoning).
245 This dual nature recalls the distinction between apocalyptic roosters and anti-apocalyptic owls, drawn by Landes 2011, pp. 37–61.

https://doi.org/10.1515/9783112230114-006

ton. Other methods for postponing the inevitable end were direct supplication to God and the exegetical technique of typology. Typology decelerates time by recalibrating the reader's attention to the quasi-repetitive pattern of multiple instantiations, which are conducive to a provisionary deferral of the end. Chapter Three reconstructed prominent exegetical typologies and showed how the chronological sequence of apocalyptic events was transcended by typological reasoning, which emulates divine synchronicity.

When taken together, the three approaches of chronology, velocity, and typology convey a coherent substructure of apocalyptic time.[246] No marked deviation from this substructure is observable in the surveyed sources.[247] Accordingly, the vector of apocalyptic time is chronologically sequenced and typologically structured. It is conditioned by the juxtaposition of urgency *and* delay and is replete with events and characters of equivocal significance and value. As noted in the introduction, Byzantine apocalyptica are inherently ambivalent. An ostensible hero is readily turned into an inveterate villain by inverting his axiological value.[248] Ambivalence defines the semantics in the grammar of the apocalyptic imagination.

Another important aspect in the grammar of apocalyptic literature pertains to verbal forms. The vast majority of the verbs stand in the future tense or aorist subjunctive, which are phonologically indistinguishable and semantically congruent—both denoting futurity. The persistent focus on the future and the abundance of temporal conjunctions provide a diachronic account. The diachronicity is temporarily suspended by the present indicative and the aorist imperative that are frequently interjected in historical apocalyptica.[249] The present-tense intermis-

246 Anachronisms and chronological inconsistencies cease to be unintelligible if read in the context of a theology of history that posits a supratemporal unity. See Kemp 1991, pp. 49–50 and Baun 2007, pp. 217–222.

247 Byzantine apocalyptica do not suggest any competitive coexistence of temporal regimes. On the notion of concurrent and competitive temporal regimes, see Edelstein, Geroulanos, and Wheatley 2020, who engage with and challenge Reinhart Koselleck's sediments of time (*Zeitschichten*).

248 The same ambivalence has been observed by Kazhdan 1995 in the domain of miracles. Evil miracles were viewed as deceptively similar to beneficial miracles. Holy and unholy wonders were indiscernible without knowledge of the miracle-worker's internal disposition. "Ambivalence", Kazhdan (Kazhdan 1995, p. 82) concludes, "was a typical feature of the Byzantine […] world view". With regard to eschatology, Gurevich 1972, p. 116 (translation in Gurevich 1985, p. 128) remarks that the Eastern Romans' eschatological outlook was inherently ambivalent, involving both fervent hope for salvation and profound dread over punishment.

249 Two examples should suffice for illustration. The *Last Vision of Daniel* contains 132 conjugated verbs (in H. Schmoldt's edition). 100 verbs express futurity (standing either in the future

sions are most often reserved for God's intervention and direct speech. They express the divine perspective of the immutable, eternal present, which operates independently from sequential order.[250] Moreover, the present-tense interjections lend vitality and immediacy to the narrative. They express simultaneity with the reader (or listener).[251] The consistent application of those specific verbal forms supports the reader's impression that, on the one hand, otherworldly atemporality is synchronous and presentist in nature and, on the other, instances of divine synchronicity proliferate as the *eschaton* approaches.

The epicenter of Byzantine apocalypses rests with the present. The various revisions and translations of those texts attest to their continuous application and broad appeal, which stemmed less from historical accuracy than from the abiding pertinence of the typological patterns, which confer meaning on the ever-escalating present. The presentist focus fostered a view of the future as contingent, open-ended, and negotiable. To navigate favorably the present meant to recognize, negotiate, and act on the continuous soteriological markers, revealed in typological manifestations. Hence, the significance of the *vaticinia ex eventu*, which provided not only auctorial legitimacy but also guided the audience along historiographical clues to the present moment. In this respect the often-ambiguous character of *vaticinia* only facilitated their pertinence. The conglomeration of diverse typologies further reinforced the presentist focus. While rooted in the historical past and pointing to the eschatological future, typologies were focused on the author's present.[252] Their proleptic frame of reference sanctified (or nullified) any given proposition or prospect. The *synteleia* was significant precisely because it infused contemporary issues with meaning and value.

---

indicative or aorist subjunctive, or employing the periphrastic construction with μέλλω), 10 are in the present tense, 16 in the aorist imperative, 4 in the aorist indicative, 1 aorist optative, and 1 in the perfect. The *Anonymous Prediction* holds 109 conjugated verbs (in A. Vassiliev's edition). 95 verbs are formed in the future indicative or aorist subjunctive, 3 stand in the aorist indicative (referring back to Old Testament events), 2 are given in the aorist imperative (directly addressing the reader), and 9 are in the present tense. In both narratives, the present tense is reserved for direct speech and general conditions.

250 A similar observation is made by Baun 2000, p. 258 and Baun 2007, pp. 144–147, who maintains that the shifts in verbal tenses that moral apocalypses regularly employ are a deliberate literary device to convey the notion of the eternal present, in which no regulated temporal succession exists. Cf. Nikolova 2011, p. 22, who argues that *Revelation* uses specific verbal tenses to express particular truth claims: the present tense expresses timeless truths, the future tense signifies changeability, and the past tense suggests predetermined facts.

251 de Jong and Nünlist 2007b, p. 521 observe that present-tense insertions "create[] the impression that the narrative is simultaneous, which increases its vividness".

252 A comparable observation is made by Betancourt 2016 with regard to Byzantine iconography. The presentist outlook existed already in *Revelation*, as shown by Yarbro Collins 2021.

In short, the presentist character of Byzantine apocalyptica is conveyed by a series of literary devices. Verbal interjections, typological patterns, fluctuations in the narrative speed, and the chronometric anomaly of the shortening of the days all qualify the apparent temporal monotony of apocalyptic narratives. These elements disrupt diachronic temporality, both phenomenologically and objectively, and converge it towards its antithesis: the continuous, synchronous present.

Apocalyptic time anticipates the transformation of diachronic mutability into synchronous stasis. The *Apocalypse of Leo of Constantinople* offers a good witness, stating that "[a]ll will resurrect at one age, all indistinguishable, all thirty years of age, they will recognize nothing in each other on account of their [outward] appearance [...] but by the clear-sighted eye of the soul [...] And then all will be raised equal [...]".[253] Existence in the post-apocalyptic, otherworldly realm was envisioned as a coetaneous condition, in which time-related disparities, such as age, are absent.[254] This coetaneous inertia was expected to be preceded by the irregularity, contraction, and eventual collapse of natural time. The alternating rhythm of narrative speed and the shortening of days clearly express this conviction. Temporal acceleration was seen as a sure sign of the impending end. High and irregular velocity unravels diachronic time and gives way to the eternal present of the afterlife. Analogously, typologies engender a sense of divine synchronicity, achieved by integrating historical instantiations of timeless types. In sum, the literary technique of narrative speed, the motif of time compression, and the exegetical method of typology all serve to facilitate the transition from dissipative time into immutable stasis.

---

253 *ApcLeonConst* §22, ll. 613–622: πάντες ἀναστήσονται μίᾳ ἡλικίᾳ, ὅλοι ἰσοκέφαλοι, ὅλοι τριάκοντα ἐτῶν, οὐδὲν γνωρίζουσιν ἀλλήλοις ἐπὶ τῇ αὐτῇ θεωρίᾳ [...] ἀλλὰ ἀπὸ διορατικὸν ὄμμα τῆς ψυχῆς· [...] καὶ τότε ἐγερθήσονται ὅλοι ἴσοι [...]. – The notion of coetaneity can also be found in *ApcIoh* §§10–11 (pp. 78–79) – *VisNiph* §90 (p. 221, ll. 18–19): Ὑπῆρχον δὲ πάντες τῇ ἡλικίᾳ ὡσεὶ τριῶν ἐτῶν. | All were about three years of age. – It is not critical whether the exact age of the resurrected is three years—as in V. Marinis' edition—or thirty years—as in the edition by Rystenko 1928, p. 98, l. 24 as well as in *ApcIoh* §10 (p. 78) and *ApcLeonConst* §22, ll. 614–615. What matters is the homogeneity of the age. Cf. *ApcAndr* ll. 2970–78, which describes the eighth age (αἰών) as an "incompletable and boundless" (ἀσυντέλεστος καὶ ἀπέραντος) extension devoid of alteration. The notion that life after death is ageless and unchanging was a common belief, which appears also outside apocalyptic literature, for instance, in the twelfth-century satire *Timarion*, see Ps-Lucianus, *Tim.* §30 (ll. 757–760).

254 The notion of a post-mortem stasis can already be found in patristic writing. See, for instance, Gregorius Nazianzenus, *In seip.* p. 252, ll. 7–10 (*Orat.* 26.11) and Maximus Confessoris, *Ambig. ad Ioan.* 10.33 (p. 278). Cf. Keller 1996, p. 101, who likens the post-apocalyptic state to a "frozen" condition.

A salient implication of apocalyptic temporality was its inhibition of cardinal innovation. No new ideology or technological progress seemed necessary in view of the typologically (re)constructed series of future events. Typology is a flexible device that allows for correction by re-instantiating (i. e., duplicating) a particular type as needed. This is apparent in the multiplication of the Savior-Emperor in middle Byzantine prophecies. Apocalyptists, who were steeped in typological exegesis, added new types or further instantiations to account for any historical shift, just as astronomers, who adhered to Ptolemaic geocentrism, used epicycles to explain any anomalous motion of the heavenly bodies. Typological exegesis could be readily used to account for unforeseen change. It could also be weaponized to denounce the personal shortcomings of any emperor or patriarch. This versatile applicability generated a sense of confidence that—coupled with imperial censorship and societal traditionalism—was prohibitive of questioning the legitimacy of the imperial and ecclesiastical institutions themselves. We have no record that Byzantine apocalyptica ever attempted to subvert the patriarchate or the imperial office as an *institution.*[255] The apocalyptic tradition discouraged radical reform—be it political, institutional, or social—and, in its stead, promoted the restoration of the already achieved.[256] The typological semiosphere achieved a level of semiotic saturation that obviated structural innovation. In a sense, it was too effective to need to innovate. As a result, the apocalyptic conception of time was both critical and reactionary in intention. It was retrospective and proleptic in orientation, sequential yet flexible in order, diachronic and synchronous in structure. Apocalyptic time was an inherently ambivalent notion in Byzantium, which left much—but not unlimited—room for historical interpretation and literary maneuver.

---

255 Byzantium never produced a Joachim of Fiore or Martin Luther, who challenged the episcopal see as an institution. On Joachimism, see the seminal work by Reeves 1969. According to Kemp 1991, pp. 66–104, it was Luther's identification of the Papacy with the Antichrist that sparked modern historiography.

256 Podskalsky 1972, p. 102, Podskalsky 1984, p. 445, Brandes 1991, p. 58, Magdalino 1993, p. 3. Cf. Betancourt 2016, p. 200, who notes that the Eastern Romans considered time to be in a constant state of fulfillment. Change, in this view, was the result of typological evolution, which precluded the need for any genuine innovation. Similarly, Gurevich 1972, pp. 112, 118 (translation in Gurevich 1985, pp. 124, 130).

Bibliography

Abbreviations

BA	Byzantinisches Archiv
BF	*Byzantinische Forschungen*
BSGRT	Bibliotheca scriptorum Graecorum et Romanorum Teubneriana
BZ	*Byzantinische Zeitschrift*
BZNW	Beihefte zur Zeitschrift für die neutestamentliche Wissenschaft
CAG	Commentaria in Aristotelem Graeca
CAVT	Clavis apocryphorum Veteris Testamenti
CPG	Clavis Patrum Graecorum
CCSG	Corpus Christianorum series Graeca
CCSL	Corpus Christianorum series Latina
CFHB	Corpus fontium historiae Byzantinae
CSCO	Corpus scriptorum Christianorum Orientalium
CSEL	Corpus scriptorum ecclesiasticorum Latinorum
DOML	Dumbarton Oaks Medieval Library
DOP	*Dumbarton Oaks Papers*
DOS	Dumbarton Oaks Studies
GCS	Die griechischen christlichen Schriftsteller der ersten Jahrhunderte
OCA	Orientalia Christiana analecta
OLA	Orientalia Lovaniensia analecta
PLP	Prosopographisches Lexikon der Palaiologenzeit
REB	*Revue des études byzantines*
SC	Sources chrétiennes
SVTP	Studia in Veteris Testamenti pseudepigrapha
TCSV	Trends in Classics, supplementary volumes
TM	*Travaux et mémoires*

Apocalyptic sources

AenigLeon (Aenigmata Leonis; Ps-Leonine Oracles), ed. Trapp, Erich (1964). "Vulgärorakel aus Wiener Handschriften." In Johannes Koder and Erich Trapp (eds), *Ἀκροθίνια. Sodalium seminarii byzantini Vindobonensis Herberto Hunger oblata.* Vienna: Institut für Byzantinistik der Universität Wien, pp. 83–120.

AnonymVatic (Anonymi vaticinium; Anonymous Prediction), ed. Vassiliev, Athanasius (1893). *Anecdota Graeco-Byzantina, pars prior.* Moscow: Universitas Caesarea, pp. 47–50.

ApcAnast (Apocalypsis Anastasiae; Apocalypse of Anastasia), ed. Homburg, Rudolf (1903). *Apocalypsis Anastasiae.* Leipzig: Teubner.

ApcAndr (Apocalypsis Andreae Sali; Apocalypse of Andrew the Fool), ed. Rydén, Lennart (1995). *The Life of St Andrew the Fool*, 2 vols. Studia Byzantina Upsaliensia 4. Uppsala: Almqvist & Wiksell, II, pp. 258–284.

https://doi.org/10.1515/9783112230114-007

ApcIoh (Apocalypsis Iohannis apocrypha; Apocryphal Apocalypse of John), ed. von Tischendorf, Konstantin (1866). *Apocalypses apocryphae Mosis, Esdrae, Pauli, Iohannis, item Mariae dormitio, additis evangeliorum et actuum apocryphorum supplementis.* Leipzig: Hermann Mendelssohn, pp. 70 – 94.

ApcLeonConst (Leonis Constantinopolitani De fine mundi homilia; Apocalypse of Leo of Constantinople), ed. Maisano, Riccardo (1975). *L'apocalisse apocrifa di Leone di Costantinopoli.* Nobiltà dello spirito, nuova serie 3. Naples: Morano Editore, pp. 67 – 116.

ApcMarVir (Apocalypsis Mariae Virginis; Apocalypse of the Theotokos), ed. James, Montague R. (1893). *Apocrypha anecdota. A collection of thirteen apocryphal books and fragments.* Texts and studies 2/3. Cambridge: Cambridge University Press, pp. 115 – 126.

ApcMeth I (Apocalypsis Methodii Graeca [redactio prima]; Apocalypse of Ps-Methodios), ed. Aerts, Willem J., and George A. A. Kortekaas (1998). *Die Apokalypse des Pseudo-Methodius. Die ältesten griechischen und lateinischen Übersetzungen, Vol. 1.* CSCO 569. Leuven: Peeters, pp. 70 – 198.

ApcMeth II (Apocalypsis Methodii Graeca [redactio secunda]; Apocalypse of Ps-Methodios), ed. Lolos, Anastasios (1976). *Die Apokalypse des Ps.Methodios.* Beiträge zur klassischen Philologie 83. Meisenheim am Glan: Anton Hain, pp. 47 – 141.

ApcMeth III (Apocalypsis Methodii Graeca [redactio tertia]; Apocalypse of Ps-Methodios), ed. Lolos, Anastasios (1978). *Die dritte und vierte Redaktion des Ps.Methodios.* Beiträge zur klassischen Philologie 94. Meisenheim am Glan: Anton Hain, pp. 22 – 75.

ApcMeth IV (Apocalypsis Methodii Graeca [redactio quarta]; Apocalypse of Ps-Methodios), ed. Lolos, Anastasios (1978). *Die dritte und vierte Redaktion des Ps.Methodios.* Beiträge zur klassischen Philologie 94. Meisenheim am Glan: Anton Hain, pp. 23, 39 – 69, 76 – 78.

DiegDan (Diegesis Danielis; Diegesis of Daniel), ed. Berger, Klaus (1976). *Die griechische Daniel-Diegese. Eine altkirchliche Apokalypse. Text, Übersetzung und Kommentar.* Studia post-biblica 27. Leiden: Brill, pp. 12 – 23.

ExposDan I (Expositio Danielis; Prophecy of Daniel), ed. Sakel, Dean (2006). "A Daniel apocalypse attributed to Methodius of Patara." In Kayhan Dörtlük, Burhan Varkıvanç, Tarkan Kahya, et al. (eds), *III. Likya sempozyumu, 7 – 10 Kasım 2005, Antalya, Sempozyum bildirileri, Vol. 2.* Antalya: Suna-İnan Kıraç Akdeniz Medeniyetleri Araştırma Enstitüsü, pp. 665 – 678, at 673 – 678.

IntrpGenSch (Interpretatio litterarum Gennadii Scholarii; Oracular interpretation of Ps-Gennadios Scholarios), ed. Vereecken, Jeannine, and Lydie Hadermann-Misguich (2000). *Les Oracles de Léon le Sage illustrés par Georges Klontzas. La version Barozzi dans le Codex Bute.* Oriens Graecolatinus 7. Venice: Institut Hellénique de Venise/Bibliothèque Vikelaia d'Hérakleion, pp. 134 – 136.

NarrMend (Narratio mendici regis; Tale of the True Emperor), ed. Brokkaar, Walter G., et al. (2002). *The Oracles of the Most Wise Emperor Leo & the Tale of the True Emperor (Amstelodamensis graecus VI E 8).* Amsterdam: Universiteit van Amsterdam, pp. 90 – 100.

OracLeon (Oracula Leonis Sapientis; Oracles of Leo the Wise), ed. Brokkaar, Walter G., et al. (2002). *The Oracles of the Most Wise Emperor Leo & the Tale of the True Emperor (Amstelodamensis graecus VI E 8).* Amsterdam: Universiteit van Amsterdam, pp. 56 – 88.

PraedAndritz (Praedictio Andritzopouli; Prediction of Andritzopoulos), ed. Rigo, Antonio (2002). "La profezia di Cosma Andritzopoulos." In Anna di Benedetto Zimbone and Francesca Rizzo Nervo (eds), *Κανίσκιν. Studi in onore di Giuseppe Spadaro.* Medioevo romanzo e orientale, studi 12. Soveria Mannelli: Rubbettino, pp. 195 – 201.

Ps-Chrys (Iohannis Chrysostomi visio Danielis; Vision of Daniel by Ps-Chrysostom), ed. Schmoldt, Hans (1972). *Die Schrift 'Vom jungen Daniel' und 'Daniels letzte Vision'*. PhD dissertation. Hamburg, pp. 220 – 236.

SepVisDan (Septima visio Danielis; Seventh Vision of Daniel), ed. Kalemkiar, Gregoris (1892). "Die siebente Vision Daniels." *Wiener Zeitschrift für die Kunde des Morgenlandes* 6, pp. 109 – 136.

SibTibGr (Sibylla Tiburtina Graeca; Oracle of Baalbek), ed. Alexander, Paul (1967). *The Oracle of Baalbek. The Tiburtine Sibyl in Greek dress.* DOS 10. Washington, DC: Dumbarton Oaks, pp. 9 – 22.

UltVisDan I (Ultima visio Danielis; Last Vision of Daniel), ed. Schmoldt, Hans (1972). *Die Schrift 'Vom jungen Daniel' und 'Daniels letzte Vision'*. PhD dissertation. Hamburg, pp. 122 – 144.

UltVisDan II (Ultima visio Danielis; Last Vision of Daniel), ed. Stephanitzēs, Petros D. (1838). *Συλλογὴ διαφόρων προρρήσεων.* Athens: A. Ἀγγελίδης, pp. 45 – 51.

VaticBrys (Vaticinium Brysonis; Prediction of Ps-Brysōn), ed. Pertusi, Agostino (1988). *Fine di Bisanzio e fine del mondo. Significato e ruolo storico delle profezie sulla caduta di Costantinopoli in Oriente e in Occidente.* Edited by Enrico Morini. Istituto storico italiano per il Medio Evo, Nuovi studi storici 3. Rome: Nella sede dell'Istituto Palazzo Borromini, pp. 162 – 166.

VatResCon I (Vaticinium de restitutione Constantinopoleos; Prophecy on the Restoration of Constantinople), ed. Kraft, András (2022). "Vaticinium de restitutione Constantinopoleos (BHG 1875b): edition and translation of a post-Byzantine prophecy." *Byzantine and Modern Greek Studies* 46/2, pp. 214 – 235, at 222 – 224.

VisDanSanHom (Visiones Danielis et aliorum sanctorum hominum; Visions of Daniel and Other Holy Men), ed. Pertusi, Agostino (1988). *Fine di Bisanzio e fine del mondo. Significato e ruolo storico delle profezie sulla caduta di Costantinopoli in Oriente e in Occidente.* Edited by Enrico Morini. Istituto storico italiano per il Medio Evo, Nuovi studi storici 3. Rome: Nella sede dell'Istituto Palazzo Borromini, pp. 172 – 201.

VisDanSepCol I (Visio Danielis de septem collibus; Vision of Daniel on the Seven Hills), ed. Schmoldt, Hans (1972). *Die Schrift 'Vom jungen Daniel' und 'Daniels letzte Vision'*. PhD dissertation. Hamburg, pp. 190 – 198.

VisDanSepCol II (Visio Danielis de septem collibus; Vision of Daniel on the Seven Hills), ed. Klostermann, Erich (1895). *Analecta zur Septuaginta, Hexapla und Patristik.* Leipzig: A. Deichert, p. 121.

VisEnoch (Visio Iusti Henoch; Vision of Enoch the Just), ed. Hovsēp'eants', Sargis (1896). *Անկանոն գիրք Հին Կտակարանաց* [*Apocryphal books of the Old Testament*]. Թանգարան հին եւ նոր նախնեաց [Museum of ancient and modern ancestors] 1. Venice: Ս. Ղազար, pp. 378 – 386.

VisioDan (Visio Danielis de tempore novissimo et de fine mundi; Vision of Daniel on the Last Times), ed. Schmoldt, Hans (1972). *Die Schrift 'Vom jungen Daniel' und 'Daniels letzte Vision'*. PhD dissertation. Hamburg, pp. 202 – 218.

VisNiph (Visio Niphonis; Vision of Niphon), ed. Marinis, Vasileios (2017). "The vision of the last judgment in the Vita of Saint Niphon (BHG 1371z)." *DOP* 71, pp. 193 – 227, at 203 – 227.

Miscellaneous primary sources

Anastasius Sinaita, *Hex.* (Hexaemeron; Commentary on Genesis), ed. Kuehn, Clement A., and John D. Baggarly (2007). *Anastasius of Sinai: Hexaemeron.* OCA 278. Rome: Pontificio Istituto Orientale.

Anastasius Sinaita, *Quaest.* (Quaestiones et responsiones; Questions and Answers), ed. Richard, Marcel, and Joseph A. Munitiz (2006). *Anastasii Sinaitae Quaestiones et responsiones.* CCSG 59. Turnhout: Brepols.

Andreas Caesariensis, *In Apoc.* (Commentarius in Apocalypsin; Commentary on Revelation), ed. Schmid, Josef (1955). *Studien zur Geschichte des griechischen Apokalypse-Textes. 1. Teil. Der Apokalypse-Kommentar des Andreas von Kaisareia. Text.* Münchner theologische Studien, 1. Ergänzungsband. Munich: Karl Zink.

Anna Comnena, *Alex.* (Alexias; Alexiad), ed. Reinsch, Diether R., and Athanasios Kambylis (2001). *Annae Comnenae Alexias, Vol. 1.* CFHB 40/1. Berlin/New York: Walter de Gruyter.

Anonymus, *Contr. Const.* (Contra Constantinopolitanos; Against the Constantinopolitans), ed. Allen, Pauline, and Bronwen Neil (1999). *Scripta saeculi VII vitam Maximi Confessoris illustrantia.* CCSG 39. Turnhout: Brepols, pp. 230–232.

Arethas, *In Apoc.* (Commentarius in Apocalypsin; Commentary on Revelation), ed. Cramer, John A. (1840). *Catena in epistolas catholicas, accesserunt Œcumenii et Arethæ commentarii in Apocalypsin.* Catenae Graecorum Patrum in Novum Testamentum 8. Oxford: Typographeum Academicum.

Barn. Epist. (Barnabae epistula; Epistle of Barnabas), ed. Holmes, Michael W., Joseph B. Lightfoot, and John R. Harmer (2007). *The Apostolic Fathers: Greek texts and English translations.* Third edition. Grand Rapids: Baker Academic, pp. 380–440.

Demetrius, *Epist.* (Epistula; Letter), ed. Darrouzès, Jean (1964). "Lettres de 1453." *REB* 22, pp. 72–127, at 90–92.

Eusebius, *De laud. Const.* (De laudibus Constantini; In the Praise of Constantine), ed. Heikel, Ivar A. (1902). *Eusebius Werke, Vol. 1. Über das Leben Constantins, Constantins Rede an die Heilige Versammlung, Tricennatsrede an Constantin.* GCS 7. Leipzig: J. C. Hinrichs, pp. 193–259.

Eusebius, *Hist. eccl.* (Historia ecclesiastica; Church History), ed. Schwartz, Eduard, Theodor Mommsen, and Friedhelm Winkelmann (1999). *Eusebius Werke, Vol. 2.2. Die Kirchengeschichte.* Zweite Auflage. GCS, Neue Folge 6. Berlin: Akademie Verlag.

Eusebius, *Vit. Const.* (Vita Constantini; Life of Constantine), ed. Winkelmann, Friedhelm (2008). *Eusebius Werke, Vol 1.1. Über das Leben des Kaisers Konstantin.* Zweite Auflage. GCS. Berlin/New York: Walter de Gruyter.

Georgius Eleusius, *VitTheoSyc* (Vita Theodori Syceotae; Life of Theodōros of Sykeōn), ed. Festugière, André-Jean (1970). *Vie de Théodore de Sykéôn, Vol. 1 : texte grec.* Subsidia hagiographica 48. Bruxelles: Société des Bollandistes.

Georgius Pisides, *In Heracl.* (In Heraclium ex Africa redeuntem; On Herakleios' return from Africa), ed. Pertusi, Agostino (1959). *Giorgio di Pisidia. Poemi, Vol. 1. Panegirici epici.* Ettal: Buch-Kunstverlag, pp. 77–81.

Germanus, *Historia myst.* (Historia mystica ecclesiae catholicae; Mystical history of the catholic church), ed. Meyendorff, Paul (1999). *On the Divine Liturgy: Germanus of Constantinople.* Crestwood: St Vladimir's Seminary Press.

Gregorius Nazianzenus, *In seip.* (In seipsum; On himself), ed. Mossay, Justin (1981). *Grégoire de Nazianze. Discours 24–26.* SC 284. Paris: Éditions du Cerf, pp. 224–272.

Hesychius, *Patr. Const.* (Patria Constantinopoleos; Patria of Constantinople), ed. Preger, Theodor (1907). *Scriptores originum Constantinopolitanarum, Vol. 2.* Leipzig: Teubner.

Hieronymus, *Epist. 77* (Epistula 77; Letter 77), ed. Hilberg, Isidor (1912). *S. Eusebii Hieronymi opera. Epistularum pars II. Epistulae LXXI–CXX.* CSEL 55. Vienna/Leipzig: F. Tempsky/G. Freytag, pp. 37 – 49.

Hieronymus, *In Hiezech.* (Commentarius in Hiezechielem; Commentary on Ezekiel), ed. Glorie, François (1964). *S. Hieronymi presbyteri opera. Pars I. Opera exegetica 4. Commentariorum in Hiezechielem libri XIV.* CCSL 75. Turnhout: Brepols.

Hippolytus, *De Christ. et Antichrist.* (De Christo et Antichristo; On Christ and the Antichrist), ed. Athanasopoulos, Panagiōtis C. (2013). *Ιππολύτου Ρώμης Περί του Αντιχρίστου – Κριτική έκδοση.* PhD dissertation. Ioannina, pp. 136 – 194.

Hippolytus, *In Dan.* (Commentarius in Danielem; Commentary on Daniel), ed. Bonwetsch, Nathanael, and Marcel Richard (2000). *Hippolyt Werke. Erster Band, erster Teil. Kommentar zu Daniel.* GCS, Neue Folge 7. Berlin: Akademie Verlag.

Hippolytus (Ps-), *De consum.* (De consummatione mundi; On the end of the world), ed. Athanasopoulos, Panagiōtis C. (2016). *Ψ.-Ιππολύτου Περὶ τῆς συντελείας τοῦ κόσμου – Κριτική έκδοση. 2η έκδοση (Ps.-Hippolytus' De consummatione mundi – A critical edition. 2nd edition).* Bibliotheca Graecorum et Romanorum 6. Ioannina: Carpe Diem, pp. 75 – 116.

Ioannis Caminiatae, *De expug.* (De expugnatione Thessalonicae; On the capture of Thessaloniki), ed. Böhlig, Gertrud (1973). *Ioannis Caminiatae De expugnatione Thessalonicae.* CFHB 4. Berlin/New York: Walter de Gruyter.

Ioannis Chrysostomus, *Comm. in Jerem.* (Commentaria in Jeremiam; Commentary on Jeremiah), ed. Migne, Jacques-Paul (1860). *Patrologia Graeca, Vol. 64.* Paris: J.-P. Migne, cols. 740B–1037B.

Ioannis Damascinus, *De haer.* (Liber de haeresibus; On heresies), ed. Kotter, Bonifatius (1981). *Die Schriften des Johannes von Damaskos, Vol. 4. Liber de haeresibus. Opera polemica.* Patristische Texte und Studien 22. Berlin/New York: Walter de Gruyter, pp. 19 – 67.

Leo Diaconus, *Hist.* (Historia; History), ed. Hase, Charles B. (1828). *Leonis Diaconi Caloënsis Historiae libri decem.* CSHB 11. Bonn: Weber.

Maximus Confessoris, *Ambig. ad Ioan.* (Ambigua ad Ioannem; Ambigua to John), ed. Constas, Nicholas (2014). *Maximos the Confessor. On difficulties in the Church Fathers: the Ambigua, Vol. 1.* DOML 28. Cambridge, MA: Harvard University Press, pp. 62 – 450.

Maximus Confessoris, *Rel. mot.* (Relatio motionis; Record of the trial), ed. Allen, Pauline, and Bronwen Neil (1999). *Scripta saeculi VII vitam Maximi Confessoris illustrantia.* CCSG 39. Turnhout: Brepols, pp. 12 – 51.

Nicephorus Blemmydes, *Epit. phys.* (Epitome physica; Compendium on Physics), ed. Migne, Jacques-Paul (1863). *Patrologia Graeca, Vol. 142.* Paris: J.-P. Migne, cols. 1024B–1320C.

Nicetas Choniates, *Hist.* (Historia; History), ed. van Dieten, Jan L. (1975). *Nicetae Choniatae Historia, Vol. 1.* CFHB 11/1. Berlin/New York: Walter de Gruyter.

Nicetas Choniates, *Orat.* (Orationes; Orations), ed. van Dieten, Jan L. (1972). *Nicetae Choniatae orationes et epistulae.* CFHB 3. Berlin/New York: Walter de Gruyter.

Nicetas David Paphlagonius, *Epist.* (Epistula ad episcopos occidentales; Letter to the Western Bishops), ed. Westerink, Leendert G. (1975). "Nicetas the Paphlagonian on the end of the world." In *Μελετήματα στη μνήμη Βασιλείου Λαούρδα. Essays in memory of Basil Laourdas.* Thessaloniki: E. Sfakianakis & Sons, pp. 177 – 195, at 191 – 195.

Nicolaus Cabasilas, *Orat.* (Orationes de visione Hiezechielis; Orations on Ezekiel's vision), ed. Pseftonkas, Basileios S. (2006). *Νικολάου Καβάσιλα Λόγοι (εισαγωγή, κείμενα, σχόλια).* Thessaloniki: Κυρομάνος, pp. 63 – 100.

Oecumenius, *In Apoc.* (Commentarius in Apocalypsin; Commentary on Revelation), ed. de Groote, Marc (1999). *Oecumenii Commentarius in Apocalypsin.* Traditio exegetica *Graeca* 8. Leuven: Peeters.

Origenes, *Hom. Num. XX* (In Numeros homilia XX; Homily 20 on Numbers), ed. Doutreleau, Louis (2001). *Origène. Homélies sur les Nombres, Vol. 3. Homélies XX–XXVIII.* SC 461. Paris: Éditions du Cerf, pp. 14–54.

Philippus Solitarius, *Diopt.* (Dioptra Philippi Monotropi; Dioptra of Philip the Monk), ed. Lavriōtēs, Spyridōn (1920). *Ἡ Διόπτρα.* Ὁ Ἄθως, Ἁγιορειτικὸν περιοδικόν 1. Athens: Π. Λ. Βεργιανίτης.

Photius, *Bibl.* (Bibliotheca; Library), ed. Henry, René (1959–1977). *Photius. Bibliothèque,* 8 vols. Collection byzantine. Paris: Les Belles Lettres.

Ps-Lucianus, *Tim.* (Timarion; Timarion), ed. Romano, Roberto (1974). *Pseudo-Luciano, Timarione. Testo critico, introduzione, traduzione, commentario e lessico.* Byzantina et Neo-Hellenica Neapolitana 2. Naples: Università di Napoli, Cattedra di Filologia Bizantina.

Quinisext. (Canones Quinisextae Sinodi in Trullo; Canons of the Quinisext Council in Trullo), ed. Ohme, Heinz (2013). *Concilium Constantinopolitanum a. 691/2 in Trullo habitum (Concilium Quinisextum).* Acta Conciliorum Oecumenicorum, II, 2/4. Berlin/Boston: Walter de Gruyter, pp. 17–86.

Romanus Melodus, *Hymn.* (Cantica; Hymns), ed. Grosdidier de Matons, José (1981). *Romanos Le Mélode. Hymnes, Vol. 5.* SC 283. Paris: Éditions du Cerf.

Simplicius, *In Arist. Phys.* (Commentarius in Aristotelis Physicorum libros; Commentary on Aristotle's Physics), ed. Diels, Hermann (1895). *Simplicii in Aristotelis Physicorum libros quattuor posteriores commentaria, Vol. 2.* CAG 10. Berlin: Reimer.

Symeon Neotheologus, *Orat.* (Orationes ethicae; Ethical Orations), ed. Darrouzès, Jean (1966). *Syméon le Nouveau Théologien. Traités théologiques et éthiques, Vol. 1.* SC 122. Paris: Éditions du Cerf, pp. 170–440.

Symeon Seth, *Consp.* (Conspectus rerum naturalium; On the Things of Nature), ed. Delatte, Armand (1939). *Anecdota Atheniensia et alia, Vol. 2 : textes grecs relatifs à l'histoire des sciences.* Bibliothèque de la Faculté de Philosophie et Lettres de l'Université de Liége 88. Liège: Faculté de Philosophie et Lettres, pp. 17–89.

Tzetzes, *Epist.* (Epistulae; Letters), ed. Leone, Pietro L. (1972). *Ioannis Tzetzae Epistulae.* BSGRT. Leipzig: Teubner.

Tzetzes, *Hist.* (Historiae; Histories), ed. Leone, Pietro L. (1968). *Ioannis Tzetzae Historiae.* Pubblicazioni dell'Istituto di Filologia Classica 1. Naples: Libreria Scientifica Editrice.

Secondary literature

Aerts, Willem J., and George A. A. Kortekaas (1998). *Die Apokalypse des Pseudo-Methodius. Die ältesten griechischen und lateinischen Übersetzungen*, 2 vols. CSCO 569–570. Leuven: Peeters.

Agamben, Giorgio (2001). *Infanzia e storia. Distruzione dell'esperienza e origine della storia.* Revised edition. Torino: Giulio Einaudi.

Ahrweiler, Hélène (1996). "Eusebius of Caesarea and the imperial Christian idea." In Avner Raban and Kenneth G. Holum (eds), *Caesarea Maritima: a retrospective after two millennia.* Documenta et monumenta Orientis antiqui 21. Leiden: Brill, pp. 541–546.

Al-Azmeh, Aziz (2004). "God's chronography and dissipative time: vaticinium ex eventu in classical and medieval Muslim apocalyptic traditions." *The Medieval History Journal* 7/2, pp. 199–225.

Alexander, Paul (1962). "The strength of empire and capital as seen through Byzantine eyes." *Speculum* 37/3, pp. 339 – 357.

Alexander, Paul (1967). *The Oracle of Baalbek. The Tiburtine Sibyl in Greek dress.* DOS 10. Washington, DC: Dumbarton Oaks.

Alexander, Paul (1968). "Medieval apocalypses as historical sources." *American Historical Review* 73/4, pp. 997 – 1018.

Alexander, Paul (1973). "Les débuts des conquêtes arabes en Sicile et la tradition apocalyptique byzantino-slave." *Bollettino. Centro di Studi Filologici e Linguistici Siciliani* 12, pp. 7 – 37.

Alexander, Paul (1985). *The Byzantine apocalyptic tradition.* Edited by Dorothy deF. Abrahamse. Berkeley: University of California Press.

Allen, Pauline, and Bronwen Neil (2002). *Maximus the Confessor and his companions: documents from exile.* Oxford early Christian texts. Oxford: Oxford University Press.

Anderson, Benjamin (2014). "Public clocks in late antique and early medieval Constantinople." *Jahrbuch der Österreichischen Byzantinistik* 64, pp. 23 – 32.

Angelov, Dimiter (2007). *Imperial ideology and political thought in Byzantium, 1204 – 1330.* Cambridge: Cambridge University Press.

Angenendt, Arnold (1998). "Die liturgische Zeit: zyklisch und linear." In Hans-Werner Goetz (ed.), *Hochmittelalterliches Geschichtsbewußtsein im Spiegel nichthistorischer Quellen.* Berlin: Akademie Verlag, pp. 101 – 115.

Auerbach, Erich (1938). "Figura." *Archivum Romanicum* 22, pp. 436 – 489.

Auerbach, Erich (1946). *Mimesis. Dargestellte Wirklichkeit in der abendländischen Literatur.* Bern: A. Francke Verlag.

Auerbach, Erich (1984). "Figura." In Erich Auerbach, *Scenes from the drama of European literature.* Theory and history of literature 9. Minneapolis: University of Minnesota Press, pp. 9 – 76.

Averintsev, Sergej S. (1975). "Порядок космоса и порядок истории в мировоззрении раннего средневековья." In Lidia A. Freiberg (ed.), *Античность и Византия.* Moscow: Наука, pp. 266 – 285.

Baetens, Jan, and Kathryn Hume (2006). "Speed, rhythm, movement: a dialogue on K. Hume's article 'narrative speed'." *Narrative* 14/3, pp. 349 – 355.

Bakhtin, Mikhail (1975). *Вопросы литературы и эстетики. Исследования разных лет.* Moscow: Художественная литература.

Bakhtin, Mikhail (1981). *The dialogic imagination. Four essays.* Transl. Caryl Emerson and Michael Holquist. Austin: University of Texas Press.

Barnes, Timothy D. (1981). *Constantine and Eusebius.* Cambridge, MA: Harvard University Press.

Barr, James (1962). *Biblical words for time.* Studies in biblical theology 33. London: SCM Press.

Bauckham, Richard (1977). "The eschatological earthquake in the Apocalypse of John." *Novum Testamentum* 19/3, pp. 224 – 233.

Baun, Jane (2000). "The moral apocalypse in Byzantium." In Albert I. Baumgarten (ed.), *Apocalyptic time.* Studies in the history of religions 86. Leiden: Brill, pp. 241 – 267.

Baun, Jane (2007). *Tales from another Byzantium: celestial journey and local community in the Medieval Greek apocrypha.* Cambridge: Cambridge University Press.

Bennema, Cornelis (2025). *Imitation in early Christianity: mimesis and religious-ethical formation.* Grand Rapids: Eerdmans.

Ben-Sasson, Menahem (2022). "'The Vision of Daniel' from the St. Petersburg Genizah." *Harvard Theological Review* 115/3, pp. 331 – 362.

Ben-Sasson, Menahem (2024). “An interreligious ‘encounter’ in four Visions of Daniel.” In Omer Michaelis and Sabine Schmidtke (eds), *Religious and intellectual diversity in the Islamicate world and beyond, Vol. 2. Essays in honor of Sarah Stroumsa.* Islamic history and civilization, studies and texts 205 – 2. Leiden/Boston: Brill, pp. 614 – 644.

Ben-Sasson, Menahem (2026). *Time and revelation in the Vision of Daniel from the St. Petersburg Collection.* Chronoi 11. Berlin: Walter de Gruyter.

Berger, Klaus (1976). *Die griechische Daniel-Diegese. Eine altkirchliche Apokalypse. Text, Übersetzung und Kommentar.* Studia post-biblica 27. Leiden: Brill.

Betancourt, Roland (2016). “Prolepsis and anticipation: the apocalyptic futurity of the now, East and West.” In Michael A. Ryan (ed.), *A companion to the premodern apocalypse.* Brill's companions to the Christian tradition 64. Leiden/Boston: Brill, pp. 177 – 205.

Betz, Otto (1963). “Der Katechon.” *New Testament Studies* 9, pp. 276 – 291.

Bonura, Christopher J. (2025). *A prophecy of empire: the Apocalypse of Pseudo-Methodius from late antique Mesopotamia to the global medieval imagination.* Christianity in Late Antiquity. Oakland: University of California Press.

Boudreau, Peter M. (2023). *Keeping time: temporal imagery and thought in the calendars of later Byzantium.* PhD dissertation. Montreal.

Bousset, Wilhelm (1895). *Der Antichrist in der Überlieferung des Judentums, des neuen Testaments und der alten Kirche. Ein Beitrag zur Auslegung der Apocalypse.* Göttingen: Vandenhoeck & Ruprecht.

Bousset, Wilhelm (1899). “Beiträge zur Geschichte der Eschatologie.” *Zeitschrift für Kirchengeschichte* 20/3, pp. 261 – 290.

Boxall, Ian K. (2023). “Israel's scriptures in the Revelation of John.” In Matthias Henze and David Lincicum (eds), *Israel's scriptures in early Christian writings: the use of the Old Testament in the New.* Grand Rapids: Eerdmans, pp. 555 – 576.

Bracke, Raphaël (1980). Ad Sancti Maximi vitam. Studie van de biografische documenten en de levensbeschrijvingen betreffende Maximus Confessor (ca. 580 – 662). PhD dissertation. Leuven.

Brandes, Wolfram (1990). “Die apokalyptische Literatur.” In Friedhelm Winkelmann and Wolfram Brandes (eds), *Quellen zur Geschichte des frühen Byzanz (4.–9. Jahrhundert). Bestand und Probleme.* Berliner byzantinistische Arbeiten 55. Amsterdam: J. C. Gieben, pp. 305 – 322, 367 – 370.

Brandes, Wolfram (1991). “Endzeitvorstellungen und Lebenstrost in mittelbyzantinischer Zeit (7.–9. Jahrhundert).” In *Varia III.* Ποικίλα Βυζαντινά 11. Bonn: Dr. Rudolf Habelt GmbH, pp. 9 – 62.

Brandes, Wolfram (1997). “Anastasios ὁ δίκορος: Endzeiterwartung und Kaiserkritik in Byzanz um 500 n. Chr.” *BZ* 90/1, pp. 24 – 63.

Brandes, Wolfram (2000). “Liudprand von Cremona (Legatio cap. 39 – 41) und eine bisher unbeachtete west-östliche Korrespondenz über die Bedeutung des Jahres 1000 a.D.” *BZ* 93/2, pp. 435 – 463.

Brandes, Wolfram (2003). “Sieben Hügel. Die imaginäre Topographie Konstantinopels zwischen apokalyptischem Denken und moderner Wissenschaft.” *Rechtsgeschichte* 2, pp. 58 – 71.

Brandes, Wolfram (2005). “Der Fall Konstantinopels als apokalyptisches Ereignis.” In Sebastian Kolditz and Ralf C. Müller (eds), *Geschehenes und Geschriebenes. Studien zu Ehren von Günther S. Henrich und Klaus-Peter Matschke.* Leipzig: Eudora-Verlag, pp. 453 – 469.

Brandes, Wolfram (2007). “Konstantinopels Fall im Jahre 1204 und ‘apokalyptische’ Prophetien.” In Wout J. van Bekkum, Jan Willem Drijvers, and Alex C. Klugkist (eds), *Syriac polemics: studies in honour of Gerrit Jan Reinink.* OLA 170. Leuven: Peeters, pp. 239 – 259.

Brandes, Wolfram (2008). "Kaiserprophetien und Hochverrat. Apokalyptische Schriften und Kaiservaticinien als Medium antikaiserlicher Propaganda." In Wolfram Brandes and Felicitas Schmieder (eds), *Endzeiten: Eschatologie in den monotheistischen Weltreligionen.* Millennium-Studien 16. Berlin/New York: Walter de Gruyter, pp. 157–200.

Brandes, Wolfram (2011). "Endzeiterwartung im Jahre 1009 a.D.?" In Thomas Pratsch (ed.), *Konflikt und Bewältigung: die Zerstörung der Grabeskirche zu Jerusalem im Jahre 1009.* Millennium-Studien 32. Berlin: Walter de Gruyter, pp. 301–320.

Brandes, Wolfram (2013). "Cento of the true emperor." In David Thomas and Alex Mallett (eds), *Christian-Muslim relations: a bibliographical history, Vol. 5 (1350–1500).* History of Christian-Muslim relations 20. Leiden/Boston: Brill, pp. 330–333.

Brandes, Wolfram (2021a). "Traditions and expectations in the medieval Eastern Christian world." In Matthias Heiduk, Klaus Herbers, and Hans-Christian Lehner (eds), *Prognostication in the medieval world: a handbook, Vol. 1.* Berlin/Boston: Walter de Gruyter, pp. 284–299.

Brandes, Wolfram (2021b). "Byzantine predictions of the end of the world in 500, 1000, and 1492 AD." In Hans-Christian Lehner (ed.), *The end(s) of time(s): apocalypticism, messianism, and utopianism through the ages.* Prognostication in history 6. Leiden/Boston: Brill, pp. 32–63.

Brandes, Wolfram (2024). "The marvelous year 692 – a hub of historical processes." In Wolfram Brandes, Helmut Reimitz, and Jack Tannous (eds), *Legal pluralism and social change in Late Antiquity and the Middle Ages. A conference in honor of John Haldon.* Studien zur europäischen Rechtsgeschichte 337. Frankfurt am Main: Vittorio Klostermann, pp. 175–228.

Brandes, Wolfram (2026). "Das sog. Constans-Vaticinium und seine Datierung. Eschatologische Vorstellungen in der ersten Hälfte des 7. Jahrhunderts?" In Mehmetcan Akpınar and Federico Montinaro (eds), *Rethinking conquest: studies on the late antique Near East from Byzantium to Islam.* Millennium-Studien 116. Berlin/Boston: Walter de Gruyter, pp. 79–120.

Breed, Brennan W. (2014). "History of reception." In Carol A. Newsom, with Brennan W. Breed, *Daniel: a commentary.* The Old Testament library. Louisville: Westminster John Knox Press, pp. 85–97.

Brokkaar, Walter G., et al. (2002). *The Oracles of the Most Wise Emperor Leo & the Tale of the True Emperor (Amstelodamensis graecus VI E 8).* Amsterdam: Universiteit van Amsterdam.

Callahan, John F. (1948). *Four views of time in ancient philosophy.* Cambridge, MA: Harvard University Press.

Caspary, Gerard E. (1979). *Politics and exegesis: Origen and the two swords.* Berkeley/Los Angeles: University of California Press.

Çelik, Siren (2023). "Some observations on notions of time in the histories of Georgios Pachymeres and Nikephoros Gregoras." *Tarih ve Coğrafya Araştırmaları Dergisi* 9/2, pp. 47–68.

Cereti, Carlo G. (1995). *The Zand ī Wahman Yasn: a Zoroastrian apocalypse.* Serie Orientale Roma 35. Rome: Istituto Italiano per il Medio ed Estremo Oriente.

Cherchi, Paolo A. (1976). "Tradition and topoi in medieval literature." *Critical Inquiry* 3/2, pp. 281–294.

Ciolfi, Lorenzo M. (2018). "Changing the rhythm to change the society: narrative time in the Life of John Vatatzes (BHG 933)." In Charis Messis, Margaret Mullet, and Ingela Nilsson (eds), *Storytelling in Byzantium: narratological approaches to Byzantine texts and images.* Studia Byzantina Upsaliensia 19. Uppsala: Uppsala Universitet, pp. 159–176.

Collins, John J. (1979). "Introduction: towards the morphology of a genre." *Semeia* 14, pp. 1–20.

Collins, John J. (1996). "Apocalyptic literature." In Paul J. Achtemeier (ed.), *The HarperCollins Bible dictionary.* Revised edition. San Francisco: HarperSanFrancisco, p. 39.

Congourdeau, Marie-Hélène (2001). "Jérusalem et Constantinople dans la littérature apocalyptique." In Michel Kaplan (ed.), *Le sacré et son inscription dans l'espace à Byzance et en Occident : études comparées.* Byzantina Sorbonensia 18. Paris: Publications de la Sorbonne, pp. 125–136.

Congourdeau, Marie-Hélène (2018). "Ézéchiel, prophète de l'économie du Sauveur: trois opuscules de Nicolas Cabasilas." *REB* 76, pp. 137–166.

Constas, Nicholas (2001). "'To sleep, perchance to dream': the middle state of souls in patristic and Byzantine literature." *DOP* 55, pp. 91–124.

Cook, David (2002). *Studies in Muslim apocalyptic.* Studies in Late Antiquity and early Islam 21. Princeton: Darwin Press.

Cook, David (2017). *'The Book of Tribulations': the Syrian Muslim apocalyptic tradition. An annotated translation by Nuʿaym b. Ḥammād al-Marwazī.* Edinburgh studies in Islamic apocalypticism and eschatology. Edinburgh: Edinburgh University Press.

Corke-Webster, James (2019). *Eusebius and empire: constructing Church and Rome in the Ecclesiastical History.* Cambridge: Cambridge University Press.

Cotsonis, Joachim (2013). "To invoke or not to invoke. The image of Christ on Byzantine lead seals. That is the question." *Revue numismatique* 170, pp. 549–582.

Cullmann, Oscar (1962). *Christus und die Zeit. Die urchristliche Zeit- und Geschichtsauffassung.* Third edition. Zurich: EVZ-Verlag.

Cupane, Carolina (2014). "The heavenly city: religious and secular visions of the other world in Byzantine literature." In Christine Angelidi and George T. Calofonos (eds), *Dreaming in Byzantium and beyond.* Farnham/Burlington, VT: Ashgate, pp. 53–68.

Dagron, Gilbert (1981). "Quand la terre tremble..." *TM* 8, pp. 87–103.

Dagron, Gilbert (1984). *Constantinople imaginaire : études sur le recueil des 'Patria'.* Bibliothèque byzantine 8. Paris: Presses Universitaires de France.

Dagron, Gilbert (1996). *Empereur et prêtre : étude sur le 'césaropapisme' byzantin.* Bibliothèque des histoires. Paris: Gallimard.

Daniélou, Jean (1948). "La typologie millenariste de la semaine dans le Christianisme primitif." *Vigiliae Christianae* 2/1, pp. 1–16.

Daniélou, Jean (1950). *Sacramentum futuri : études sur les origines de la typologie biblique.* Études de théologie historique. Paris: Beauchesne.

Davidson, Richard M. (1981). *Typology in Scripture: a study of hermeneutical τύπος structures.* Andrews University seminary doctoral dissertation series 2. Berrien Spring, MI: Andrews University Press.

Davidson, Richard M. (2011). "The eschatological hermeneutic of biblical typology." *TheoRhēma* 6/2, pp. 5–48.

Dawes, Elizabeth, and Norman H. Baynes (1948). *Three Byzantine saints. Contemporary biographies translated from the Greek.* Oxford: Basil Blackwell.

Debié, Muriel (2024). *Alexandre le Grand en syriaque: le maître des lieux, des savoirs et des temps.* Bibliothèque de l'Orient chrétien 7. Paris: Les Belles Lettres.

de Jong, Irene J.F., and René Nünlist (2007a). "Introduction. Narratological theory on time." In Irene J.F. de Jong and René Nünlist (eds), *Time in ancient Greek literature. Studies in ancient Greek narrative, Vol. 2.* Mnemosyne, Bibliotheca classica Batava 291. Leiden/Boston: Brill, pp. 1–14.

de Jong, Irene J.F., and René Nünlist (2007b). "Time in ancient Greek literature." In Irene J.F. de Jong and René Nünlist (eds), *Time in ancient Greek literature. Studies in ancient Greek narrative, Vol. 2.* Mnemosyne, Bibliotheca Classica Batava 291. Leiden/Boston: Brill, pp. 505–522.

de Lange, Nicholas (2007). "Jewish and Christian messianic hopes in pre-Islamic Byzantium." In Markus Bockmuehl and James C. Paget (eds), *Redemption and resistance: the messianic hopes of Jews and Christians in Antiquity.* London/New York: T&T Clark, pp. 274–284.

Delouis, Olivier (2003). "Topos et typos, ou les dessous vétérotestamentaires de la rhétorique hagiographique à Byzance aux VIIIe–IXe siècles." *Hypothèses* 6, pp. 235–248.

Demandt, Alexander (2015). *Zeit. Eine Kulturgeschichte.* Berlin: Propyläen.

Denson, Ryan (2022). "Procopius and the Lord of the Demons: the synthesis of the demonic Justinian." *Journal of Late Antiquity* 15/2, pp. 494–518.

Dillenberger, John (1986). *A theology of artistic sensibilities: the visual arts and the Church.* New York: Crossroad.

Dimant, Devorah (2001). *Qumran Cave 4, XXI: parabiblical texts, part 4. Pseudo-prophetic texts.* Discoveries in the Judaean Desert 30. Oxford: Clarendon Press.

DiTommaso, Lorenzo (2005). *The Book of Daniel and the apocryphal Daniel literature.* SVTP 20. Leiden/Boston: Brill.

Eco, Umberto (1998). "À toutes fins utiles." In Jean-Claude Carrière, Jean Delumeau, Umberto Eco, et al., *Entretiens sur la fin des temps.* Paris: Fayard, pp. 235–295.

Edelstein, Dan, Stefanos Geroulanos, and Natasha Wheatley (2020). "Chronocenosis: an introduction to power and time." In Dan Edelstein, Stefanos Geroulanos, and Natasha Wheatley (eds), *Power and time: temporalities in conflict and the making of history.* Chicago/London: University of Chicago Press, pp. 1–49.

Erdeljan, Jelena (2017). *Chosen places: constructing New Jerusalems in Slavia Orthodoxa.* East Central and Eastern Europe in the Middle Ages, 450–1450, 45. Leiden/Boston: Brill.

Flannery-Dailey, Frances (1999). "Non-linear time in apocalyptic texts: the spiral model." *Society of Biblical Literature – 1999 seminar papers.* Atlanta: Society of Biblical Literature, pp. 231–245.

Flower, Richard (2019). "Witnesses for the persecution: textual communities of exile under Constantius II." *Studies in Late Antiquity* 3/3, pp. 337–368.

Frye, Northrop (1982). *The great code: the Bible and literature.* New York/London: Harcourt Brace Jovanovich.

Gador-Whyte, Sarah (2017). *Theology and poetry in early Byzantium: the Kontakia of Romanos the Melodist.* Cambridge: Cambridge University Press.

Garstad, Benjamin (2012). *Apocalypse of Pseudo-Methodius. An Alexandrian World Chronicle.* DOML 14. Cambridge, MA: Harvard University Press.

Genette, Gérard (1972). *Figures III.* Paris: Éditions du Seuil.

Geppert, Alexander C.T., and Till Kössler (2015). "Zeit-Geschichte als Aufgabe." In Alexander C.T. Geppert and Till Kössler (eds), *Obsession der Gegenwart. Zeit im 20. Jahrhundert.* Göttingen: Vandenhoeck & Ruprecht, pp. 7–36.

Gil, Juan (1992). "Der zyklische Gedanke im eschatologischen Glauben der Spätantike und des Mittelalters." In Dieter Hertel and Jürgen Untermann (eds), *Andalusien zwischen Vorgeschichte und Mittelalter.* Forum Ibero-Americanum 7. Cologne: Böhlau, pp. 139–190.

Goppelt, Leonhard (1964). "Apokalyptik und Typologie bei Paulus." *Theologische Literaturzeitung* 89/5, pp. 321–344.

Goppelt, Leonhard (1966). *Typos. Die typologische Deutung des Alten Testaments im Neuen.* Beiträge zur Förderung christlicher Theologie, ser. 2, 43. Darmstadt: Wissenschaftliche Buchgesellschaft.

Greisiger, Lutz (2014). *Messias – Endkaiser – Antichrist. Politische Apokalyptik unter Juden und Christen des Nahen Ostens am Vorabend der arabischen Eroberung.* Orientalia Biblica et Christiana 21. Wiesbaden: Harrassowitz.

Greisiger, Lutz (2016). "Opening the gates of the north in 627: war, anti-Byzantine sentiment and apocalyptic expectancy in the Near East prior to the Arab invasion." In Wolfram Brandes, Felicitas Schmieder, and Rebekka Voß (eds), *Peoples of the apocalypse: eschatological beliefs and political scenarios.* Millennium-Studien 63. Berlin/Boston: Walter de Gruyter, pp. 63–79.

Greisiger, Lutz (2017). "The end is coming – to what end? Millenarian expectations in the seventh-century Eastern Mediterranean." In Hagit Amirav, Emmanouela Grypeou, and Guy Stroumsa (eds), *Apocalypticism and eschatology in Late Antiquity: encounters in the Abrahamic religions, 6th–8th centuries.* Late antique history and religion 17. Leuven: Peeters, pp. 87–106.

Grumel, Venance (1958). *La chronologie.* Traité d'études byzantines 1. Paris: Presses Universitaires de France.

Grypeou, Emmanouela (2013). "Ephraem Graecus, 'Sermo in adventum Domini': a contribution to the study of the transmission of apocalyptic motifs in Greek, Latin and Syriac traditions in Late Antiquity." In Samir K. Samir and Juan P. Monferrer-Sala (eds), *Graeco-Latina et Orientalia: studia in honorem Angeli Urbani heptagenarii.* Series Syro-Arabica 2. Cordoba: Oriens Academic, pp. 165–179.

Grypeou, Emmanouela, and Helen Spurling (2013). *The Book of Genesis in Late Antiquity: encounters between Jewish and Christian exegesis.* Jewish and Christian perspectives series 24. Leiden/Boston: Brill.

Guinot, Jean-Noël (1989). "La typologie comme technique herméneutique." In *Figures de l'Ancien Testament chez les Pères.* Cahiers de Biblia Patristica 2. Strasbourg: Centre d'Analyse et de Documentation Patristiques, pp. 1–34.

Guran, Petre (2014). "Historical prophecies from late antique apocalypticism to secular eschatology." *Revue des études sud-est européennes* 52, pp. 47–62.

Gurevich, Aaron J. (1972). *Категории средневековой культуры.* Moscow: Издательство Искусство.

Gurevich, Aaron J. (1985). *Categories of medieval culture.* Transl. George L. Campbell. London: Routledge and Kegan Paul.

Gutierrez, Cathy (2005). "The millennium and narrative closure." In Stephen D. O'Leary and Glen S. McGhee (eds), *War in heaven/heaven on earth: theories of the apocalyptic.* Millennialism and society 2. London/Oakville, CT: Equinox, pp. 47–59.

Hatzopoulos, Marios (2009). "From resurrection to insurrection: 'sacred' myths, motifs, and symbols in the Greek War of Independence." In Roderick Beaton and David Ricks (eds), *The making of modern Greece: nationalism, romanticism, and the uses of the past (1797–1896).* Farnham/Burlington, VT: Ashgate, pp. 81–93.

Hatzopoulos, Marios (2011). "Oracular prophecy and the politics of toppling Ottoman rule in South-East Europe." *The Historical Review / La Revue Historique* 8, pp. 95–116.

Himmelfarb, Martha (2017). *Jewish messiahs in a Christian empire: a history of the Book of Zerubbabel.* Cambridge, MA: Harvard University Press.

Holdenried, Anke (2017). "The old made new: medieval repurposing of prophecies." In Sibylle Baumbach, Lena Henningsen, and Klaus Oschema (eds), *The fascination with unknown time.* Cham: Palgrave Macmillan, pp. 23–41.

Homan, Roger (2006). *The art of the sublime: principles of Christian art and architecture.* Aldershot/ Burlington, VT: Ashgate.

Hultgård, Anders (1998). "Persian apocalypticism." In John J. Collins (ed.), *The encyclopedia of apocalypticism, Vol. 1: the origins of apocalypticism in Judaism and Christianity.* New York: Continuum, pp. 39 – 83.

Hultgård, Anders (1999). "The Vision of Enoch the Just and medieval apocalypses." In Valentina Calzolari Bouvier, Jean-Daniel Kaestli, and Bernard Outtier (eds), *Apocryphes arméniens : transmission, traduction, création, iconographie. Actes du colloque international sur la littérature apocryphe en langue arménienne (Genève, 18 – 20 septembre 1997).* Lausanne: Éditions du Zèbre, pp. 147 – 158.

Hume, Kathryn (2005). "Narrative speed in contemporary fiction." *Narrative* 13/2, pp. 105 – 124.

Humphreys, Michael T. G. (2015). *Law, power, and imperial ideology in the iconoclast era, c. 680 – 850.* Oxford studies in Byzantium. Oxford: Oxford University Press.

Iser, Wolfgang (1971). "Indeterminacy and the reader's response in prose fiction." In Joseph Hillis Miller (ed.), *Aspects of narrative: selected papers from the English Institute.* New York/London: Columbia University Press, pp. 1 – 45.

Issaverdens, Jacques (1901). *The uncanonical writings of the Old Testament found in the Armenian mss. of the library of St. Lazarus.* Venice: Armenian Monastery of St. Lazarus.

Istrin, Vasilij (1897). *Откровенiе Мефодiя Патарскаго и апокрифическiя видѣнiя Даніила въ византiйской и славяно-русской литературахъ: изслѣдованiе и тексты*, 2 vols. Moscow: Университетская типографiя.

Jenks, Gregory C. (1991). *The origins and early development of the Antichrist myth.* BZNW 59. Berlin/ New York: Walter de Gruyter.

Jensen, Robin M. (2019). "Ritual and early Christian art." In Risto Uro, Juliette J. Day, Richard E. DeMaris, et al. (eds), *The Oxford handbook of early Christian ritual.* Oxford: Oxford University Press, pp. 587 – 609.

Kaegi, Walter E. (2000). "Gigthis and Olbia in the Pseudo-Methodius Apocalypse and their significance." *BF* 26, pp. 161 – 167.

Kaldellis, Anthony (2022). "Alexander the Great in Byzantine tradition, AD 330 – 1453." In Richard Stoneman (ed.), *A history of Alexander the Great in world culture.* Cambridge: Cambridge University Press, pp. 216 – 241.

Kampers, Franz (1896). *Die deutsche Kaiseridee in Prophetie und Sage.* Munich: Lüneburg.

Kannengiesser, Charles (2004). *Handbook of patristic exegesis: the Bible in ancient Christianity, Vol. 1.* Leiden/Boston: Brill.

Kazhdan, Alexander (1995). "Holy and unholy miracle workers." In Henry Maguire (ed.), *Byzantine magic.* Washington, DC: Dumbarton Oaks, pp. 73 – 82.

Kazhdan, Alexander (1999). *A history of Byzantine literature (650 – 800).* National Hellenic Research Foundation, Institute for Byzantine Research, Research Series 2. Athens: Εθνικό Ίδρυμα Ερευνών.

Kazhdan, Alexander (2006). *A history of Byzantine literature (850 – 1000).* Edited by Christine Angelidi. National Hellenic Research Foundation, Institute for Byzantine Research, Research Series 4. Athens: Εθνικό Ίδρυμα Ερευνών.

Kazhdan, Alexander, and Giles Constable (1982). *People and power in Byzantium. An introduction to modern Byzantine studies.* Washington, DC: Dumbarton Oaks.

Keller, Catherine (1996). *Apocalypse now and then: a feminist guide to the end of the world.* Boston: Beacon Press.

Kemp, Anthony (1991). *The estrangement of the past: a study in the origins of modern historical consciousness.* New York/Oxford: Oxford University Press.

Koder, Johannes (2016). *Die Byzantiner. Kultur und Alltag im Mittelalter.* Vienna: Böhlau Verlag.

Koder, Johannes (2019). "Time as a dimension of Byzantine identity." *Studia Ceranea* 9, pp. 523 – 542.

Kosmin, Paul J. (2018). *Time and its adversaries in the Seleucid Empire.* Cambridge, MA: Harvard University Press.

Kotoula, Dimitra (forthcoming). "'For the sake of God, arise': politics and eschatology in the Chora burial chapel." In Athanasios Semoglou and Natalia Poulou (eds), *Re(dis)covering Chora: the Byzantine Name of the Rose. Proceedings from the International Symposium, Thessaloniki, 25 – 26 November 2021.* Thessaloniki: Ευρωπαϊκό Κέντρο Βυζαντινών και Μεταβυζαντινών Μνημείων.

Kountoura-Galakē, Eleōnora (2001). "Προρρήσεις μοναχών και ανάδειξη αυτοκρατόρων στη διάρκεια των 'σκοτεινών αιώνων'." In Eleōnora Kountoura-Galakē (ed.), *Οι σκοτεινοί αιώνες του Βυζαντίου (7ος–9ος αι.).* Διεθνή συμπόσια 9. Athens: Εθνικό Ίδρυμα Ερευνών, pp. 421 – 441.

Kraft, András (2012). "The last roman emperor topos in the Byzantine apocalyptic tradition." *Byz* 82, pp. 213 – 257.

Kraft, András (2017). "Living on the edge of time: temporal patterns and irregularities in Byzantine historical apocalypses." In Sibylle Baumbach, Lena Henningsen, and Klaus Oschema (eds), *The fascination with unknown time.* Cham: Palgrave Macmillan, pp. 71 – 91.

Kraft, András (2018a). "An inventory of Medieval Greek apocalyptic sources (c. 500 – 1500 AD): naming and dating, editions and manuscripts." *Millennium-Jahrbuch* 15, pp. 69 – 143.

Kraft, András (2018b). "Miracles and pseudo-miracles in Byzantine apocalypses." In Maria Gerolemou (ed.), *Recognizing miracles in Antiquity and beyond.* TCSV 53. Berlin: Walter de Gruyter, pp. 111 – 130.

Kraft, András (2018c). "Typological hermeneutics and apocalyptic time: a case study of the Medieval Greek Last Vision of the Prophet Daniel." In Elenē G. Saradē, Aikaterinē Dellaporta, and Theōnē Kollyropoulou (eds), *Όψεις του Βυζαντινού Χρόνου. Πρακτικά Διεθνούς Συνεδρίου, Αθήνα, 29 – 30 Μαΐου 2015.* Kalamata: Πανεπιστήμιο Πελοποννήσου/Χριστιανικό και Βυζαντινό Μουσείο, pp. 180 – 194.

Kraft, András (2018d). *The apocalyptic horizon in Byzantium: philosophy, prophecy, and politics during the eleventh through thirteenth centuries.* PhD dissertation. Budapest.

Kraft, András (2019). "Review of: Stephen J. Shoemaker: The apocalypse of empire. University of Pennsylvania Press, 2018." *Plekos* 21, pp. 531 – 547.

Kraft, András (2020). "Byzantine apocalyptic literature." In Colin McAllister (ed.), *The Cambridge companion to apocalyptic literature.* Cambridge companions to religion. Cambridge: Cambridge University Press, pp. 172 – 189.

Kraft, András (2021a). "Prophecies as a resource of decision-making: the case of Alexios V Doukas Mourtzouphlos' execution at the Column of Theodosios." In Michael Grünbart (ed.), *Unterstützung bei herrscherlichem Entscheiden. Experten und ihr Wissen in transkultureller und komparativer Perspektive.* Kulturen des Entscheidens 5. Göttingen: Vandenhoeck & Ruprecht, pp. 86 – 107.

Kraft, András (2021b). "Natural disasters in Medieval Greek apocalypses." *Scrinium* 17, pp. 158 – 171.

Kraft, András (2022). "Navigating the ambiguity of Byzantine apocalypses: remarks on genre, exegesis, and manuscript transmission." In Nicoletta Bruno, Giulia Dovico, Olivia Montepaone,

et al. (eds), *The limits of exactitude in Greek, Roman, and Byzantine literature and textual transmission.* TCSV 137. Berlin: Walter de Gruyter, pp. 337 – 359.

Kraft, András (2024). "Apocalyptic discourse in Nikētas Chōniatēs' History: Andronikos I Komnēnos revisited." *Études byzantines et post-byzantines, Nouvelle série*, 6 (XIII), pp. 139 – 156.

Krueger, Derek (2004). *Writing and holiness: the practice of authorship in the early Christian East.* Divinations: rereading late ancient religion. Philadelphia: University of Pennsylvania Press.

Krueger, Derek (2014). *Liturgical subjects: Christian ritual, biblical narrative, and the formation of the self in Byzantium.* Divinations: rereading late ancient religion. Philadelphia: University of Pennsylvania Press.

Kuper, Charles (2025). *The Menologion of Basil II.* DOML 89. Cambridge, MA: Harvard University Press.

Lambros, Spyridōn P. (1900). *Catalogue of the Greek manuscripts on Mount Athos, Vol. 2.* Cambridge: Cambridge University Press.

Landels, John G. (1979). "Water-clocks and time measurement in classical Antiquity." *Endeavour* 3/1, pp. 32 – 37.

Landes, Richard (2011). *Heaven on earth: the varieties of the millennial experience.* Oxford: Oxford University Press.

La Porta, Sergio (2013). "The Seventh Vision of Daniel. A new translation and introduction." In Richard Bauckham, James R. Davila, and Alexander Panayotov (eds), *Old Testament pseudepigrapha: more noncanonical scriptures, Vol. 1.* Grand Rapids: Eerdmans, pp. 410 – 434.

Lash, Ephrem (1995). *Kontakia on the Life of Christ: St. Romanos the Melodist.* The sacred literature series. San Francisco: HarperCollins Publishers.

Leach, Edmund (1972). "Melchisedech and the emperor: icons of subversion and orthodoxy." *Proceedings of the Royal Anthropological Institute of Great Britain and Ireland* 1972, pp. 5 – 14.

Le Goff, Jacques (1960). "Au Moyen Âge : temps de l'Église et temps du marchand." *Annales. Économies, sociétés, civilisations* 15/3, pp. 417 – 433.

Leroux, Jean-Marie (ed.) (1984). *Le temps chrétien de la fin de l'Antiquité au Moyen Âge, IIIe–XIIIe siècles, Paris 9 – 12 mars 1981.* Colloques internationaux du CNRS 604. Paris: Éditions du CNRS.

Lietaert Peerbolte, Bert J. (1996). *The antecedents of Antichrist: a traditio-historical study of the earliest Christian views on eschatological opponents.* Supplements to the Journal for the Study of Judaism 49. Leiden/New York: Brill.

Lolos, Anastasios (1976). *Die Apokalypse des Ps.Methodios.* Beiträge zur klassischen Philologie 83. Meisenheim am Glan: Anton Hain.

Lolos, Anastasios (1978). *Die dritte und vierte Redaktion des Ps.Methodios.* Beiträge zur klassischen Philologie 94. Meisenheim am Glan: Anton Hain.

Louth, Andrew (2009). "Space, time and the liturgy." In Adrian Pabst and Christoph Schneider (eds), *Encounter between Eastern orthodoxy and radical orthodoxy: transfiguring the world through the word.* Farnham/Burlington: Ashgate, pp. 215 – 231.

Louth, Andrew (2013). "Experiencing the liturgy in Byzantium." In Claire Nesbitt and Mark Jackson (eds), *Experiencing Byzantium: papers from the Forty-fourth Spring Symposium of Byzantine Studies, Newcastle and Durham, April 2011.* Publications of the Society for the Promotion of Byzantine Studies 18. Farnham/Burlington: Ashgate, pp. 79 – 88.

Louth, Andrew (2017). "Pope Martin I and Maximos the Confessor in their struggle for orthodoxy against the empire." *Ökumenisches Forum* 39, pp. 19 – 27.

MacCormack, Sabine G. (1982). "Christ and empire, time and ceremonial in sixth century Byzantium and beyond." *Byz* 52, pp. 287 – 309.

Magdalino, Paul (1983). "Aspects of twelfth-century Byzantine Kaiserkritik." *Speculum* 58/2, pp. 326–346.
Magdalino, Paul (1993). "The history of the future and its uses: prophecy, policy and propaganda." In Roderick Beaton and Charlotte Roueché (eds), *The making of Byzantine history. Studies dedicated to Donald M. Nicol.* Centre for Hellenic Studies, King's College London, publications 1. Aldershot/Brookfield, VT: Variorum, pp. 3–34.
Magdalino, Paul (1999). "'What we heard in the Lives of the saints we have seen with our own eyes': the holy man as literary text in tenth-century Constantinople." In James Howard-Johnston and Paul A. Hayward (eds), *The cult of saints in Late Antiquity and the Middle Ages: essays on the contribution of Peter Brown.* Oxford: Oxford University Press, pp. 83–112.
Magdalino, Paul (2000a). "Το τέλος του χρόνου στο Βυζάντιο." *Αρχαιολογία & Τέχνες* 75, pp. 23–31.
Magdalino, Paul (2000b). "The pen of the aunt: echoes of the mid-twelfth century in the Alexiad." In Thalia Gouma-Peterson (ed.), *Anna Komnene and her times.* Garland medieval casebooks 29. New York/London: Garland, pp. 15–43.
Magdalino, Paul (2002). "Une prophétie inédite des environs de l'an 965 attribuée à Léon le Philosophe (MS Karakallou 14, f. 253r–254r)." *TM* 14, pp. 391–402.
Magdalino, Paul (2003). "The year 1000 in Byzantium." In Paul Magdalino (ed.), *Byzantium in the year 1000.* The medieval Mediterranean 45. Leiden/Boston: Brill, pp. 233–270.
Magdalino, Paul (2005). "Prophecies on the fall of Constantinople." In Angeliki Laiou (ed.), *Urbs capta: the Fourth Crusade and its consequences. La IVe croisade et ses conséquences.* Réalités byzantines 10. Paris: Lethielleux, pp. 41–53.
Magdalino, Paul (2007a). "Isaac II, Saladin and Venice." In Jonathan Shepard (ed.), *The expansion of orthodox Europe: Byzantium, the Balkans and Russia.* The expansion of Latin Europe, 1000–1500. Aldershot/Burlington, VT: Ashgate, pp. 93–106.
Magdalino, Paul (2007b). "Postscript." In Jonathan Shepard (ed.), *The expansion of orthodox Europe: Byzantium, the Balkans and Russia.* The expansion of Latin Europe, 1000–1500. Aldershot/Burlington, VT: Ashgate, pp. 61–63.
Magdalino, Paul (2008). "The end of time in Byzantium." In Wolfram Brandes and Felicitas Schmieder (eds), *Endzeiten: Eschatologie in den monotheistischen Weltreligionen.* Millennium-Studien 16. Berlin/New York: Walter de Gruyter, pp. 119–133.
Magdalino, Paul (2017). "Basileia: the idea of monarchy in Byzantium, 600–1200." In Anthony Kaldellis and Niketas Siniossoglou (eds), *The Cambridge intellectual history of Byzantium.* Cambridge: Cambridge University Press, pp. 575–598.
Magdalino, Paul (2019). "Prophecy, divination and the church in Byzantium." In Paul Magdalino and Andrei Timotin (eds), *Savoirs prédictifs et techniques divinatoires de l'Antiquité tardive à Byzance.* Seyssel: La Pomme d'Or, pp. 185–202.
Magdalino, Paul (2021). "The religious rhetoric of political prophecy." In Ivan Biliarsky, Mihail Mitrea, and Andrei Timotin (eds), *Religious rhetoric of power in Byzantium and South-Eastern Europe. Proceedings of the session held at the 12th International Congress of South-East European Studies (Bucharest, 2–6 September 2019).* Brăila: Muzeul Brăilei "Carol I", pp. 11–25.
Magdalino, Paul, and Robert Nelson (2010). "Introduction." In Paul Magdalino and Robert Nelson (eds), *The Old Testament in Byzantium.* Dumbarton Oaks Byzantine symposia and colloquia. Washington, DC: Dumbarton Oaks, pp. 1–38.
Maguire, Henry (1997) "The heavenly court." In Henry Maguire (ed.), *Byzantine court culture from 829 to 1204.* Washington, DC: Dumbarton Oaks, pp. 247–258.
Mango, Cyril (1980). *Byzantium: the Empire of New Rome.* New York: Charles Scribner's Sons.

Mango, Cyril (1984). “Le temps dans les commentaires byzantins de l’Apocalypse.” In Jean-Marie Leroux (ed.), *Le temps chrétien de la fin de l’Antiquité au Moyen Âge, IIIe–XIIIe siècles, Paris 9–12 mars 1981.* Colloques internationaux du CNRS 604. Paris: Éditions du CNRS, pp. 431–438.

Marinis, Vasileios (2017). *Death and the afterlife in Byzantium: the fate of the soul in theology, liturgy, and art.* New York: Cambridge University Press.

Marsengill, Katherine (2013). *Portraits and icons: between reality and spirituality in Byzantine art.* Byzantioς 5. Turnhout: Brepols.

McGinn, Bernard (1978). “Angel pope and papal Antichrist.” *Church History* 47/2, pp. 155–173.

McGinn, Bernard (2000). *Antichrist: two thousand years of the human fascination with evil.* New York: Columbia University Press.

McKirahan, Richard (2001). *Simplicius: On Aristotle, Physics 8.6–10.* Ancient commentators on Aristotle. London: Duckworth.

Meier, Mischa (2003). *Das andere Zeitalter Justinians. Kontingenzerfahrung und Kontingenzbewältigung im 6. Jahrhundert n. Chr.* Hypomnemata 147. Göttingen: Vandenhoeck & Ruprecht.

Mesler, Katelyn (2007). “Imperial prophecy and papal crisis: the Latin reception of the Prophecy of the True Emperor.” *Rivista di storia della Chiesa in Italia* 61/2, pp. 371–415.

Metzger, Paul (2005). *Katechon: II Thess 2,1–12 im Horizont apokalyptischen Denkens.* BZNW 135. Berlin/New York: Walter de Gruyter.

Meyendorff, John (1974). *Byzantine theology: historical trends and doctrinal themes.* New York: Fordham University Press.

Meyer, Mati (2009). “The personification of Zion in Byzantine psalters with marginal illustrations: between eschatological hopes and realia.” *Ars Judaica* 5, pp. 7–22.

Möhring, Hannes (2000). *Der Weltkaiser der Endzeit. Entstehung, Wandel und Wirkung einer tausendjährigen Weissagung.* Mittelalter-Forschungen 3. Stuttgart: Jan Thorbecke.

Momigliano, Arnaldo (1982). “The origins of universal history.” *Annali della Scuola Normale Superiore di Pisa. Classe di Lettere e Filosofia, Serie III*, 12/2, pp. 533–560.

Mosshammer, Alden A. (2008). *The Easter computus and the origins of the Christian era.* Oxford early Christian studies. Oxford: Oxford University Press.

Neil, Bronwen (2006). “Narrating the trials and death in exile of Pope Martin I and Maximus the Confessor.” In John Burke (ed.), *Byzantine narrative: papers in honour of Roger Scott.* Byzantina Australiensia 16. Leiden/Boston: Brill, pp. 71–83.

Neil, Bronwen (2016). “The Theotokos as selective intercessor for souls in Middle Byzantine apocalyptic.” *Analogia. The Pemptousia Journal for Theological Studies* 1, pp. 32–42.

Newsom, Carol A. (2005). “Spying out the land: a report from genology.” In Ronald L. Troxel, Kelvin G. Friebel, and Dennis R. Magary (eds), *Seeking out the wisdom of the ancients. Essays offered to honor Michael V. Fox on the occasion of his sixty-fifth birthday.* Winona Lake: Eisenbrauns, pp. 437–450.

Nikolova, Vanya (2011). “‘Ἔπεσε, ἔπεσε Βαβυλὼν ἡ μεγάλη’ (Rev 14:8). Prophetic past or remembered future.” In Albena Milanova, Vesselina Vatchkova, and Tsvetelin Stepanov (eds), *Memory and oblivion in Byzantium / Памет и забрава във Византия.* Sofia: Военно издателство, pp. 14–23.

Ninow, Friedbert (2001). *Indicators of typology within the Old Testament: the Exodus motif.* Friedensauer Schriftenreihe A, Theologie 4. Frankfurt am Main: Peter Lang.

Ong, Walter J. (1994), “Mimesis and the following of Christ.” *Religion & Literature* 26/2, pp. 73–77.

Ostrogorsky, George (1956). “The Byzantine emperor and the hierarchical world order.” *The Slavonic and East European Review* 35, pp. 1–14.

Ozoline, Nicolas (1990). "Theology in colour: the icon of Christ' nativity." In Gennadios Limouris (ed.), *Icons: windows on eternity. Theology and spirituality in colour.* Faith and order paper 147. Geneva: WCC Publications, pp. 132–140.

Palmer, James T. (2014). *The apocalypse in the early Middle Ages.* New York: Cambridge University Press.

Paschalidēs, Symeōn A. (1999). *Νικήτας Δαβίδ Παφλαγών, το πρόσωπο και το έργο του. Συμβολή στη μελέτη της προσωπογραφίας και της αγιολογικής γραμματείας της προμεταφραστικής περιόδου.* Βυζαντινά κείμενα και μελέται 28. Thessaloniki: Κέντρο Βυζαντινών Ερευνών.

Perrin, Andrew B., and Loren T. Stuckenbruck (eds) (2021). *Four kingdom motifs before and beyond the Book of Daniel.* Themes in biblical narrative 28. Leiden/Boston: Brill.

Pertusi, Agostino (1979). "Le profezie sulla presa di Costantinopoli (1204) nel cronista veneziano Marco (c. 1292) e le loro fonti bizantine (Pseudo-Costantino Magno, Pseudo-Daniele, Pseudo-Leone il Saggio)." *Studi Veneziani*, n.s. 3, pp. 13–46.

Pertusi, Agostino (1988). *Fine di Bisanzio e fine del mondo. Significato e ruolo storico delle profezie sulla caduta di Costantinopoli in Oriente e in Occidente.* Edited by Enrico Morini. Istituto storico italiano per il Medio Evo, Nuovi studi storici 3. Rome: Nella sede dell'Istituto Palazzo Borromini.

Phrantzolas, Kōnstantinos G. (1992). *Ὁσίου Ἐφραίμ τοῦ Σύρου, ἔργα, Vol. 4.* Thessaloniki: Το Περιβόλι της Παναγίας.

Pissis, Nikolas (2014). "Apokalyptik und Zeitwahrnehmung in griechischen Texten der osmanischen Zeit." In Andreas Helmedach, Markus Koller, Konrad Petrovszky, et al. (eds), *Das osmanische Europa. Methoden und Perspektiven der Frühneuzeitforschung zu Südosteuropa.* Leipzig: Eudora-Verlag, pp. 463–486.

Pissis, Nikolas (2021). "Epistemic entanglements in seventeenth-century Books of Prophecies." In Nora Schmidt, Nikolas Pissis, and Gyburg Uhlmann (eds), *Wissensoikonomien. Ordnung und Transgression vormoderner Kulturen.* Wiesbaden: Harrassowitz, pp. 301–320.

Podskalsky, Gerhard (1972). *Byzantinische Reichseschatologie. Die Periodisierung der Weltgeschichte in den vier Grossreichen (Daniel 2 und 7) und dem tausendjährigen Friedensreiche (Apok. 20). Eine motivgeschichtliche Untersuchung.* Munich: W. Fink.

Podskalsky, Gerhard (1974). "Marginalien zur byzantinischen Reichseschatologie." *BZ* 67/2, pp. 351–358.

Podskalsky, Gerhard (1984). "Représentation du temps dans l'eschatologie impériale byzantine." In Jean-Marie Leroux (ed.), *Le temps chrétien de la fin de l'Antiquité au Moyen Âge, IIIe–XIIIe siècles, Paris 9–12 mars 1981.* Colloques internationaux du CNRS 604. Paris: Éditions du CNRS, pp. 439–450.

Podskalsky, Gerhard (1986). "La profezia di Daniele (cc. 2 e 7) negli scrittori dell'Impero romano d'Oriente." In *Popoli e spazio romano tra diritto e profezia.* Documenti e studi 3. Naples: Edizioni Scientifiche Italiane, pp. 309–320.

Podskalsky, Gerhard (1990). "Ruhestand oder Vollendung? Zur Symbolik des achten Tages in der griechisch-byzantinischen Theologie." In Günter Prinzing and Dieter Simon (eds), *Fest und Alltag in Byzanz.* Munich: Beck, pp. 157–166, 216–219.

Pogossian, Zaroui, and Sergio La Porta (2017). "Apocalyptic texts, transmission of topoi, and their multi-lingual background: the Prophecies of Agat'on and Agat'angel On the End of the World." In Lorenzo DiTommaso, Matthias Henze, and William Adler (eds), *The embroidered Bible: studies in biblical apocrypha and pseudepigrapha in honour of Michael E. Stone.* SVTP 26. Leiden/Boston: Brill, pp. 824–851.

Portier-Young, Anathea E. (2011). *Apocalypse against empire: theologies of resistance in early Judaism.* Grand Rapids: Eerdmans.

Pratsch, Thomas (2005). *Der hagiographische Topos. Griechische Heiligenviten in mittelbyzantinischer Zeit.* Millennium-Studien 6. Berlin/New York: Walter de Gruyter.

Prince, Gerald (1982). *Narratology: the form and functioning of narrative.* Janua Linguarum, series maior 108. Berlin: Mouton.

Rapp, Claudia (2010). "Old Testament models for emperors in early Byzantium." In Paul Magdalino and Robert Nelson (eds), *The Old Testament in Byzantium.* Dumbarton Oaks Byzantine symposia and colloquia. Washington, DC: Dumbarton Oaks, pp. 175–197.

Rautman, Marcus (2006). *Daily life in the Byzantine Empire.* The Greenwood Press Daily life through history series. Westport: Greenwood Press.

Reeves, John C. (1994). "An Enochic citation in Barnabas 4.3 and the Oracles of Hystaspes." In John C. Reeves and John Kampen (eds), *Pursuing the text: studies in honor of Ben Zion Wacholder on the occasion of his seventieth birthday.* Journal for the Study of the Old Testament supplement series 184. Sheffield: Sheffield Academic Press, pp. 260–277.

Reeves, Marjorie (1969). *The influence of prophecy in the later Middle Ages: a study in Joachimism.* Oxford: Clarendon Press.

Reinink, Gerrit J. (1982). "Ismael, der Wildesel in der Wüste. Zur Typologie der Apokalypse des Pseudo-Methodius." *BZ* 75, pp. 336–344.

Reinink, Gerrit J. (2002). "Heraclius, the New Alexander: apocalyptic prophecies during the reign of Heraclius." In Gerrit J. Reinink and Bernard H. Stolte (eds), *The reign of Heraclius (610–641): crisis and confrontation.* Groningen studies in cultural change 2. Leuven: Peeters, pp. 81–94.

Rigo, Antonio (1992). "L'anno 7000, la fine del mondo e l'Impero cristiano. Nota su alcuni passi di Giuseppe Briennio, Simeone di Tessalonica e Gennadio Scolario." In Giuseppe Ruggieri (ed.), *La cattura della fine. Variazioni dell'escatologia in regime di cristianità.* Testi e ricerche di scienze religiose, nuova serie 7. Genova: Marietti, pp. 151–185.

Röckelein, Hedwig (1998). "Geschichtsbewußtsein in hochmittelalterlichen Jenseitsvisionen." In Hans-Werner Goetz (ed.), *Hochmittelalterliches Geschichtsbewußtsein im Spiegel nichthistorischer Quellen.* Berlin: Akademie Verlag, pp. 143–160.

Rothauge, Caroline (2017). "Es ist (an der) Zeit. Zum 'temporal turn' in der Geschichtswissenschaft." *Historische Zeitschrift* 305, pp. 729–746.

Rubenstein, Jay (2019). "Afterword." In Matthew Gabriele and James T. Palmer (eds), *Apocalypse and reform from Late Antiquity to the Middle Ages.* London/New York: Routledge, pp. 221–228.

Rubin, Berthold (1951). "Der Fürst der Dämonen. Ein Beitrag zur Interpretation von Prokops Anekdota." *BZ* 44, pp. 469–481.

Runciman, Steven (1977). *The Byzantine theocracy.* The Weil Lectures, Cincinnati 1973. Cambridge: Cambridge University Press.

Rydén, Lennart (1978). "The date of the Life of Andreas Salos." *DOP* 32, pp. 127–155.

Rydén, Lennart (1995). *The Life of St Andrew the Fool*, 2 vols. Studia Byzantina Upsaliensia 4. Uppsala: Almqvist & Wiksell.

Rydén, Lennart (2000). "Time in the Lives of the Fools." In Cordula Scholz and Georgios Makris (eds), *Πολύπλευρος νοῦς. Miscellanea für Peter Schreiner zu seinem 60. Geburtstag.* BA 19. Munich/Leipzig: K. G. Saur, pp. 311–323.

Rystenko, Aleksandr V. (1928). *Materialien zur Geschichte der byzantinisch-slavischen Literatur und Sprache.* Odessa: Центральна-наукова бібліотека.

Sackur, Ernst (1898). *Sibyllinische Texte und Forschungen. Pseudomethodius, Adso und die Tiburtinische Sibylle.* Halle: Max Niemeyer.

Samara, Demetra (2018). "An unedited poem from codex Marcianus gr. 403." *Medioevo greco* 18, pp. 245–252.

Saradē, Elenē G., Aikaterinē Dellaporta, and Theōnē Kollyropoulou (eds) (2018). *Όψεις του Βυζαντινού Χρόνου. Πρακτικά Διεθνούς Συνεδρίου, Αθήνα, 29–30 Μαΐου 2015.* Kalamata: Πανεπιστήμιο Πελοποννήσου/Χριστιανικό και Βυζαντινό Μουσείο.

Schmidt-Biggemann, Wilhelm (2004). *Philosophia perennis: historical outlines of Western spirituality in ancient, medieval and early modern thought.* Archives internationales d'histoire des idées 189. Dordrecht: Springer.

Schott, Jeremy M. (2011). "Eusebius' Panegyric on the Building of Churches (HE 10.4.2–72): aesthetics and the politics of Christian architecture." In Sabrina Inowlocki and Claudio Zamagni (eds), *Reconsidering Eusebius: collected papers on literary, historical, and theological issues.* Supplements to Vigiliae Christianae 107. Leiden/Boston: Brill, pp. 177–197.

Schreiner, Peter (1989). "Eine chinesische Beschreibung Konstantinopels aus dem 7. Jahrhundert." *Istanbuler Mitteilungen* 39, pp. 493–505.

Scott, Roger D. (1985). "Malalas, the Secret History, and Justinian's propaganda." *DOP* 39, pp. 99–109.

Ševčenko, Ihor (2002). "Unpublished Byzantine texts on the end of the world about the year 1000 AD." *TM* 14, pp. 561–578.

Shoemaker, Stephen J. (2018). *The apocalypse of empire: imperial eschatology in Late Antiquity and early Islam.* Divinations: rereading late ancient religion. Philadelphia: University of Pennsylvania Press.

Silvano, Luigi (2025). "Literature for hard times: Palaiologan apocalyptic between tradition and innovation." In Marie-Hélène Blanchet and Raúl Estangüi Gómez (eds), *State and society in the Palaiologan era (13th–15th centuries).* Routledge research in Byzantine studies. London/New York: Routledge, pp. 223–254.

Stephenson, Paul (2003). "Anna Comnena's Alexiad as a source for the Second Crusade?" *Journal of Medieval History* 29, pp. 41–54.

Stone, Michael E., and Matthias Henze (2013). *4 Ezra and 2 Baruch: translations, introductions, and notes.* Minneapolis: Fortress Press.

Suermann, Harald (1987). "Einige Bemerkungen zu syrischen Apokalypsen des 7. Jhds." In Han J. W. Drijvers, René Lavenant, Cornelia Molenberg, et al. (eds), *IV Symposium Syriacum 1984. Literary genres in Syriac literature (Groningen – Oosterhesselen, 10–12 September).* OCA 229. Rome: Pont. Institutum Studiorum Orientalium, pp. 327–335.

Taft, Robert F. (1992). *The Byzantine rite. A short history.* American essays in liturgy series. Collegeville: Liturgical Press.

Talbot, Alice-Mary, and Denis Sullivan (2005). *The History of Leo the Deacon: Byzantine military expansion in the tenth century.* Washington, DC: Dumbarton Oaks.

Tamiōlakēs, Vasileios (2011). *Η διδασκαλία των Πατέρων της Εκκλησίας για τον Αντίχριστο (δογματική διερεύνηση).* PhD dissertation. Thessaloniki.

Torgerson, Jesse W. (2022). *The Chronographia of George the Synkellos and Theophanes. The ends of time in ninth-century Constantinople.* Brill's series on the early Middle Ages 28. Leiden/Boston: Brill.

Treadgold, Warren (2004). "The prophecies of the Patriarch Methodius." *REB* 62, pp. 229–237.

Turner, Christopher J. G. (1964). "Pages from late Byzantine philosophy of history." *BZ* 57/2, pp. 346 – 373.

van Donzel, Emeri, and Andrea Schmidt (2010). *Gog and Magog in early Eastern Christian and Islamic sources: Sallam's quest for Alexander's Wall.* Brill's Inner Asian library 22. Leiden/Boston: Brill.

Vasiliev, Alexander A. (1946). *The Russian attack on Constantinople in 860.* The Mediaeval Academy of America, publication 46. Cambridge, MA: Mediaeval Academy of America.

Vassiliev, Athanasius (1893). *Anecdota Graeco-Byzantina, pars prior.* Moscow: Universitas Caesarea.

Veselovskij, Aleksandr N. (1875). "Опыты по исторіи развитія христіанской легенды (II)." *Журналъ Министерства Народнаго Просвѣщенія* 179, pp. 48 – 130.

Vines, Michael E. (2007). "The apocalyptic chronotope." In Roland Boer (ed.), *Bakhtin and genre theory in biblical studies.* Semeia studies 63. Atlanta: Society of Biblical Literature, pp. 109 – 117.

von Dobschütz, Ernst (1903). "Coislinianus 296." *BZ* 12, pp. 534 – 567.

von Erffa, Hans M. (1995). *Ikonologie der Genesis. Die christlichen Bildthemen aus dem Alten Testament und ihre Quellen, Vol. 2.* Munich/Berlin: Deutscher Kunstverlag.

von Falkenhausen, Vera (2023). "Basilius Rex oder Rex Authari? Überlegungen zu einem passus in der 'Ὅρασις τοῦ Δανιὴλ περὶ τοῦ ἐσχάτου καιροῦ καὶ περὶ τῆς συντελείας τοῦ αἰῶνος'." In Isabel Grimm-Stadelmann, Alexander Riehle, Raimondo Tocci, et al. (eds), *Anekdota Byzantina. Studien zur byzantinischen Geschichte und Kultur. Festschrift für Albrecht Berger anlässlich seines 65. Geburtstags.* BA 41. Berlin/Boston: Walter de Gruyter, pp. 109 – 115.

Vos, Geerhardus (1948). *Biblical theology: Old and New Testaments.* Grand Rapids: Eerdmans.

White, Hayden (1973). *Metahistory: the historical imagination in nineteenth-century Europe.* Baltimore/London: Johns Hopkins University Press.

Wortley, John (1970a). "The Life of St. Andrew the Fool." In Frank L. Cross (ed.), *Studia Patristica 10. Papers presented to the Fifth International Conference on Patristic Studies held in Oxford 1967, Vol. 1.* Berlin: Akademie Verlag, pp. 315 – 319.

Wortley, John (1970b). "The warrior-emperor of the Andrew Salos Apocalypse." *Analecta Bollandiana* 88, pp. 45 – 59.

Wortley, John. (1973). "The political significance of the Andrew-Salos Apocalypse." *Byzantion* 43, pp. 248 – 263.

Wortley, John (1977). "The literature of catastrophe." *Byzantine Studies/Études byzantines* 4, pp. 1 – 17.

Yarbro Collins, Adela (2021). "Time and history: the use of the past and the present in the Book of Revelation." In Jens Schröter, Tobias Nicklas, and Armand Puig i Tàrrech (eds), *Dreams, visions, imaginations: Jewish, Christian and Gnostic views of the world to come.* BZNW 247. Berlin/Boston: Walter de Gruyter, pp. 187 – 214.

Index nominum et rerum

https://doi.org/10.1515/9783112230114-008

Index manuscriptorum

https://doi.org/10.1515/9783112230114-009

The following volumes have been published in this series:

Volume 2
Detel, Wolfgang. *Subjektive und objektive Zeit: Aristoteles und die moderne Zeit-Theorie.* Berlin/Boston: De Gruyter, 2021.

Volume 3
Singer, P. N. *Time for the Ancients: Measurement, Theory, Experience*. Berlin/Boston: De Gruyter, 2022.

Volume 4
Gertzen, Thomas L. *Aber die Zeit fürchtet die Pyramiden: Die Wissenschaften vom Alten Orient und die zeitliche Dimension von Kulturgeschichte*. Berlin/Boston: De Gruyter, 2022.

Volume 6
Zachhuber, Johannes. *Time and Soul: From Aristotle to St. Augustine*. Berlin/Boston: De Gruyter, 2022.

Volume 7
Golitsis, Pantelis. *Damascius' Philosophy of Time*. Berlin/Boston: De Gruyter, 2023.

Volume 8
Defaux, Olivier. *La Table des rois: Contribution à l'histoire textuelle des ›Tables faciles‹ de Ptolémée*. Berlin/Boston: De Gruyter, 2023.

Volume 9
Fischer, Julia (ed.). *Zwiegespräche über die Zeit: Dialoge in der Berlin-Brandenburgischen Akademie der Wissenschaften aus Anlass des sechzigsten Geburtstags von Christoph Markschies.* Berlin/Boston: De Gruyter, 2024.

Volume 10
Walter, Anke (ed.). *The Temporality of Festivals: Approaches to Festive Time in Ancient Babylon, Greece, Rome, and Medieval China*. Berlin/Boston: De Gruyter, 2024.

Volume 12
Sieroka, Norman. *Zeit-Hören: Erfahrungen, Taktungen, Musik*. Berlin/Boston: De Gruyter, 2024.

Volume 13
Birk, Ralph/Coulon, Laurent (ed.). *The Thebaid in Times of Crisis: Revolt and Response in Ptolemaic Egypt*. Berlin/Boston: De Gruyter, 2025.

Volume 14
Pallavidini, Marta. *(A)synchronic (Re)actions: Crises and Their Perception in Hittite History*. Berlin/Boston: De Gruyter, 2025.

Volume 15
Nosch, Marie-Louise Bech. *Time and Textiles in Ancient Greece*. Berlin/Boston: De Gruyter, 2025.

Volume 16
Klinger, Jörg. *Das Erfassen von Zeit im Kontext der Vergangenheit*. Berlin/Boston: De Gruyter, 2026.

Volume 17
Zachhuber, Johannes. *Time and History in Denis Pétau. Philosophy, Science, and Religion in Early Modern France*. Berlin/Boston: De Gruyter, 2026.

Volume 18
Ossendrijver, Mathieu. *Conceptions of Cyclicity in Babylonian and Greco-Roman Scholarship*. Berlin/Boston: De Gruyter, 2025.

Volume 19
Schumacher, Lydia. *From Eternal to Everlasting: God and Time in Franciscan Thought*. Berlin/Boston: De Gruyter, 2026.

Volume 20
Wiedemann, Felix. *The Modern Hammurapi: An Old Babylonian King in Imperial Germany*. Berlin/Boston: De Gruyter, 2026.

Volume 21
Niehoff, Maren R./Markschies, Christoph (eds.). *Aspects of Time in Jewish and Christian Exegesis*. Berlin/Boston: De Gruyter, 2026.

Volume 22
Korobili, Giouli/Miller, Kassandra/van der Eijk, Philip (eds.). *Synchronizing the Body in Ancient Medicine and Philosophy*. Berlin/Boston: De Gruyter, 2026.

www.ingramcontent.com/pod-product-compliance
Lightning Source LLC
LaVergne TN
LVHW010836120826
845149LV00017B/1477

* 9 7 8 3 1 1 2 2 3 0 1 0 7 *